STUCK

WHY ASIAN AMERICANS

DON'T REACH THE TOP

OF THE CORPORATE LADDER

STUCK

MARGARET M. CHIN

NEW YORK UNIVERSITY PRESS

New York

NEW YORK UNIVERSITY PRESS
New York
www.nyupress.org

References to Internet websites (URLs) were accurate at the time of writing. Neither the author nor New York University Press is responsible for URLs that may have expired or changed since the manuscript was prepared.

Library of Congress Cataloging-in-Publication Data
Names: Chin, Margaret May, 1962–   author.
Title: Stuck : why Asian Americans don't reach the top of the corporate ladder /
Margaret M. Chin.
Description: New York : New York University Press, 2020. |
Includes bibliographical references and index.
Identifiers: LCCN 2019043223 | ISBN 9781479816811 (cloth) |
ISBN 9781479842766 (paperback) | ISBN 9781479873807 (ebook) |
ISBN 9781479845682 (ebook)
Subjects: LCSH: Leadership. | Asian Americans—Education. |
Asian Americans—Psychology. | Affirmative action programs.
Classification: LCC HM1263 .C45 2020 | DDC 305.895/073—dc23
LC record available at https://lccn.loc.gov/2019043223

New York University Press books are printed on acid-free paper, and their binding materials are chosen for strength and durability. We strive to use environmentally responsible suppliers and materials to the greatest extent possible in publishing our books.

Manufactured in the United States of America

10 9 8 7 6 5 4 3 2

Also available as an ebook

To Perry, Alex, and Meredith—who keep me laughing and grounded

Contents

Introduction

AT a 2013 reception at the New York Harvard Club for newly admitted students, an event at which perhaps half of those attending appeared to be Asian Americans, because they brought their many proud relatives, an admissions officer said to me, only half joking, that since 1980 the college "had admitted and graduated thousands of second-generation Asian Americans" and added, "Where are they? Why aren't they at the top?" In other words, why weren't Asian Americans among the elite professionals in corporate America? Why weren't they occupying the so-called C-suites, the traditional province of senior executives?

Harvard's admissions team has always believed that the students admitted by the university are the cream of the crop. Based on information in alumni reunion books and other data, Harvard officials knew that virtually all of the university's second-generation Asian American graduates were employed and were by most standards doing very well professionally. But university officials expected that after about three to four decades, many more of these graduates would have attained leadership jobs in the private, public, nonprofit, and political sectors. Yet data accumulated about these graduates showed that very few of Harvard's Asian American graduates had ascended to these levels.

I ask similar questions in this book. What has become of these second-generation Asian Americans? And given their significant academic achievements, why can't more of them be found at the top levels of the business and professional worlds? Is there a so-called bamboo ceiling, an invisible but powerful barrier that halts their progress at a certain point?

Perhaps there is, because for this population the problem is not simply earning a college degree or landing an entry-level job but attaining a C-suite job, the C standing for job titles that include the word "chief."

In this book I define second-generation Asian Americans as those who were born in the United States or arrived in the country before the age of thirteen, a cohort sometimes known as the 1.5 generation. The two groups that compose this generation are socially indistinguishable from one another because all of them were raised in the United States and thoroughly Americanized by way of the school system. Those born or raised in America represent 40.1 percent of the twenty-five- to sixty-four-year-olds working full-time in the private and nonprofit sectors, according to data collected through the American Community Survey conducted by the US Census Bureau from 2013 to 2017.

Of all Asian Americans between the ages of twenty-five and sixty-four, 40.1 percent are the broadly defined second generation. And second-generation Asian Americans represent an increasing portion of younger age groups. They comprise 58.1 percent of twenty-five- to thirty-four-year-olds, 41.6 percent of thirty-five- to forty-four-year-olds, 28.7 percent of forty-five- to fifty-four-year-olds, and 19.7 percent of fifty-five- to sixty-four-year-olds.

Their general failure to attain leadership positions is evident even in fields in which Asian Americans are statistically overrepresented, notably technology. Studies of professionals in law and business indicate unexpectedly similar results. Not surprisingly, given these statistics, the so-called bamboo ceiling has in recent years been the focus of the bulk of research on Asian Americans in the workforce.[1]

Industry studies focusing on the fields of not only technology but also finance and law show the same pattern. "A Portrait of Asian Americans in the Law," a 2017 report by Eric Chung and his colleagues Samuel Dong, Xiaonan April Hu, Christine Kwon, and Goodwin Liu, published by Yale Law School and the National Asian Pacific American Bar Association, showed that despite the fact that Asian Americans have constituted the largest minority group in major law firms for nearly two decades, they have the lowest partner-to-associate ratio among all ethnic groups. At American law firms, about 90 percent of equity partners are white, whereas Asian Americans represent just 11.8 percent of associates and 3 percent of partners.[2]

In technology companies located in the San Francisco Bay Area, Asian Americans, along with other minorities, have had difficulty climbing the management ladder to become executives, despite their noticeable proficiency in technical subjects. Buck Gee, former CEO of Andiamo Systems, and Cisco GM and VP, and Denise Peck, former VP at Cisco Systems and now executive advisor with ASCEND, found that by 2015 "despite being outnumbered by Asian men and women in the entry-level professional workforce, white men and women were twice as likely as Asians to become executives and held almost three times the number of executive jobs."[3]

Similar statistics exist for Wall Street. Studies show that in finance Asian Americans make up only 12 percent of professionals and less than 5 percent of executives, wrote Laura Colby for *Bloomberg*.[4] And there are fewer than a dozen Asian CEOs in the *Fortune* 500, according to Jeff Green, Jordyn Holman, and Janet Paskin for *Bloomberg Businessweek*.[5] In an article published in May 2018 in *Harvard Business Review*, Gee and Peck point out that at Goldman Sachs, one of the world's leading financial companies, 27 percent of the American workforce was Asian American, but only 11 percent of its US executives and senior managers and none of its executive officers were Asian American.[6] Even though there are so few in the upper echelons, Asian Americans, including the foreign-born, compose almost 7 percent of the US population, more than 10 percent of the student population on most college campuses, and close to 25 percent of students at most elite college campuses.

* * *

Like the Harvard admissions officers and these studies, sociologists Richard Alba and Guillermo Yrizar Barbosa from the CUNY Graduate Center, in their 2015 *Ethnic and Racial Studies* journal article "Room at the Top?," written thirty-five years after Harvard began admitting minorities in large numbers, ask the same question: Where are the Asian Americans, especially the second generation? In response, the authors suggest that perhaps it will take more time for this generation to make its mark on the corporate world. They predict that capable Asian Americans and other minorities will move into higher-level jobs when white baby boomers retire. They contend that certain members of minority groups possess the credentials to ascend to these positions, and like many immigration scholars, they predict that as US demographics change, there will be room at the top.

Richard Zweigenhaft, a psychologist from Guilford College, and William Domhoff, a psychologist and sociologist from UC Santa Cruz, reach a different conclusion in their 2011 book *The New CEOs: Women, African American, Latino, and Asian American Leaders of Fortune 500 Companies*. They contend that the leadership of corporations—in other words the corporate elite—has opened up a bit, but that leadership positions will continue to be held largely by white men, with only a small group of elite women and nonwhite men included in their ranks.

For these scholars, demography is not destiny. In their opinion the elite class will reproduce itself with only a few exceptions to satisfy minimum expectations in a society that is at least in theory a meritocracy. However, belief in such a process is viewed by many scholars as overly simplistic. Seemingly opaque forces that affect the promotion pipeline can have an impact when it comes to achievement on both the individual and the institutional levels.

* * *

This book focuses on the professional experiences of second-generation Asian American adults and their often sputtering movement up the corporate ladder. It explores such elements as diversity and affirmative action programs designed to help advancement, and examines the points at which Asian Americans fall out of the pipeline as well as the reasons why they believe they can or cannot move up.

To examine this issue, from 2014 to 2016 I interviewed a large sample of second-generation Asian Americans who were born in the United States or arrived here before the age of age thirteen. They are defined as elites by virtue of their education (at an Ivy League or similarly prestigious institution), their income (all earned well over ninety-five thousand dollars a year), and their status (they held corporate jobs in finance, media, law, insurance, and creative technology).[7] Members of this population find it relatively easy to be hired but have considerable trouble moving to the top within an organization.

As mentioned, in an effort to explain this phenomenon, many sociologists contend that America is experiencing a period of "transition to diversity" as whites begin to retire and Asian Americans, among many different groups, become old enough and trained enough to fill leadership roles. There should be room at the top, these scholars contend, and more inclusion and diversity will be forthcoming. Just wait, they urge.

But as a sociologist, a second-generation Asian American, a first-generation college student, a beneficiary of affirmative action, a Harvard alum, a Harvard spouse, and a Harvard parent, I ask, how long does one have to wait?

I'm typical of the 1980s Chinese American cohort. My immigrant parents did not finish high school, although my dad immigrated from China at age twelve. He was fluent in English and Chinese and was a banquet waiter for most of his life. My mother also came from China, but in the 1960s, and was a garment worker for most of her life. By the time I was born in New York City, my parents had moved to Manhattan's Upper West Side to a low-income New York City Housing Authority public housing project near Lincoln Center. I attended public schools, including Stuyvesant High School, for most of my life. It was clear to me back in 1979 when I was a high school senior that Harvard was implementing affirmative action by recruiting minority students, including Asian Americans, at a Chinatown college fair. I decided to apply to Harvard only after meeting an Asian American student.

Using their affirmative action program the university made a considerable effort to send current students to college fairs across the nation to recruit young people who otherwise never would have considered Harvard. Later, as a Harvard student, I worked for the university's undergraduate minority recruitment program. When I subsequently learned the history of this program, I realized that I had been an early beneficiary of affirmative action since Asian Americans had only recently been included, within the previous five years, in the roster of groups whose members the school sought. I graduated Harvard in 1984.

Similarly, when trying to determine what career I would pursue, IBM gave me a chance to explore the many facets of their corporation. In each of my three summer IBM internships, I was placed with different divisions of the company. After graduation I worked at IBM for six years in marketing and was promoted several times before taking a sabbatical and returning to school to earn my master's and doctorate degrees at Columbia University.

During interviews conducted for this study, one respondent told me that my description of my IBM experience—the summer jobs, the rotations, the promotions, and the executive education at Wharton and even the sabbatical that IBM offered me—were all part of IBM's commitment to recruiting, training, and retaining women and members of minority groups, initiatives that were and still are part of the company's affirmative action and diversity programs. This all made sense because the 1980s was a time when many institutions were using affirmative action to increase the numbers of women and people of color in their ranks. Most people were very optimistic about the heights that women and minorities could reach in the professional world, especially with the help of affirmative action programs. In fact I testified as an amicus witness to support race-conscious admissions at Harvard in the fall of 2018.

As I was starting my career I also watched some of my peers speed through their professional careers as editors, doctors, and partners of law firms. However, I also noticed many more whose careers were stalling. By the end of the recession in 2013, a few of my friends and even younger relatives had been laid off, and it was distressing for me to see how long it took some of them to return to work.

* * *

The second generation of Asian America has become synonymous with dazzling education success. Not only are these Asian Americans among the first in their families to go to college or even graduate from high school, countless numbers of them have attended top-tier institutions.[8] This story is even more remarkable given that so many of them are the children of immigrants. Indeed, Asian Americans have been widely touted as a contemporary immigrant success story—the so-called model minority.

Yet education and the rigorous parenting that supports these children—the so-called tiger mom who pushes her children almost beyond endurance—are only part of the story of what drives success in America or of the story of individual or intergenerational mobility.[9] After college or the advanced degree comes the world of work. How do Asian American children of immigrant parents experience this critical transition from family to higher education and then into professions via various promotion ladders? And how do they understand and learn to operate the levers of success?

This book tells the seldom told story of how second-generation Asian Americans fare in the professional world and examines how their family upbringing and college and work experiences affect their trajectory in the elite corporate workforce. Attention to the multifaceted transition to adulthood of second-generation Asian Americans is long overdue. A number of these college graduates represent the elite of the Asian American second generation because a sizable number attended Ivy League colleges and other elite institutions, and have made inroads to the upper echelons of corporations and politics.

Certainly, in the opinion of the public Asian Americans are regarded as a group able to succeed in a supposedly meritocratic system through the resourcefulness and resilience that are inculcated and prized by their culture. They typically fit the model minority stereotype by skyrocketing through educational institutions and then through corporate doorways. The model minority narrative seems even more compelling given the fact that second-generation Asian Americans are so diverse in terms of their family origins; they come from upper-, middle-, and working-class families. But while this book includes examples of second-generation Asian Americans who have moved quickly up the professional ladder, they represent only a small part of the overall population.

To explore this issue, I interviewed 103 second-generation Asian Americans who graduated from college between 1980 and 2008, are in their late twenties to late fifties, and hold professional jobs. Most of the people I interviewed have worked in corporate American for over twenty years, and their experiences reveal a work world in which entrée to the upper rungs seems impossible for many and rife with racial, gender, and class inequalities that complicate and even contradict the story of the model minority's upward path. Even though these people were selected for my study by what is known as snowball sampling, an approach in which existing subjects of a study recruit future subjects from among their acquaintances, every effort was made to find individuals at midcareer or higher senior levels to determine their trajectory in the work world.

My subjects were selected because they all had jobs that required performance reviews, which were used to determine how quickly they would be promoted and how much money they would earn. I also spoke with many professional coaches and human resources workers. I attended meetings and conferences hosted by pan-Asian and professional diversity organizations such as Leadership Education for Asian Pacifics, ASCEND Pan-Asian Leaders, the National Association of Asian American Professionals (NAAAP), the Asian American Bar Association of New York, Asian Women in Business, and other work-related conferences led by organizations such as the Asia Society and the Asian American Federation of New York.

I discuss the different cohorts of the Asian American second generation as a way of explaining diversity within this demographic group. For instance, each of these cohorts has a different relationship with affirmative action and diversity programs. The oldest group was the first sizable group to graduate from college in the 1980s, and most of its members benefited from affirmative action, instituted after the 1964 Civil Rights Act to ensure greater diversity at work and in schools.[10] By 1978, even though the *Bakke* Supreme Court decision set limits on affirmative action, race was still allowed to be a factor, especially in admissions.[11]

Until the early to mid-1980s, Asian Americans, like members of many other minority groups, were rarely seen on elite college campuses. Subsequently, however, many Asian Americans, received extra consideration to bring diversity to campus, including some for being the children of laborers or the first in their families to attend college. Affirmative action programs also opened doors to college and even entry-level jobs for these Asian Americans, who represented an initial sizable wave.

The second group I look at are those who graduated from college in the 1990s, who were much more middle class and likely to have parents who had received some degree of education. Many affirmative action programs helped Asian Americans who needed them. The group itself was becoming much more diverse in terms of ethnicity, class, and parental education, and many more young Asian Americans were attending college—by 2000, 4.2 percent of the country's college-age population, aged eighteen to twenty-four, were Asian American, compared to 3.6 percent of the US population as a whole.[12]

The people I interviewed told me that corporate recruiting and training programs that selected women, minorities, and Asian Americans were still in place in the 1990s. Today, however, there are fewer programs that recruit Asian Americans, despite the need for such efforts. Those that remain include the Sponsors for Educational Opportunity, the Emma Bowen Foundation, and the Posse Foundation programs.[13]

Very few studies have examined the extent to which Asian Americans can enter the higher tiers of American professional life because most people assume that those raised in America are already executives or are simply too young to attain such positions. Since census data show that Asian Americans have the highest levels of education and highest average income among all racial groups, many people assume that they must be ascending to the highest echelons in the corporate world. Still others assume that the second generation is not old enough nor sufficiently represented in the professional world to be worth studying. In addition, most of the few studies that exist combined the broadly defined second-generation Asian Americans with the foreign-born who immigrated after age thirteen.

The earliest study, *The Glass Ceiling and Asian Americans* (to become a 2000 book with a similar name), commissioned by the US Department of Labor, was completed in 1994 by Deborah Woo, a sociologist at the University of California, Santa Cruz , and suggested that Asian Americans, including immigrants who had been educated abroad, lacked the necessary language skills and that there were specific internal structural barriers—a lack of mentors, no career development or rotational job assignments, and little or no exposure to informal networks—all of which hampered their ability to move up the corporate ladder.

Would this study have reached the same conclusions if it had examined only those Asian Americans born and raised in America? Perhaps, but probably not. Sociologist Philip Kasinitz, political scientist John Mollenkopf, sociologist Mary Waters, and co-director of a policy research center Jennifer Holdaway, in their pathbreaking 2008 study *Inheriting the City: The Children of Immigrants Come of Age*, found that it was important to include the 1.5 generation in order to understand how the children of immigrants were integrated into the larger society.

I include members of this generation because they represent a sizable number of Asian Americans, and by excluding them we would miss significant aspects of the process of mobility in the professional world. My findings indicate that when it comes to job promotions, the experiences of this population are very complicated. Members of this group are doing better than their foreign-born and -educated counterparts but not as well as many immigration scholars would have expected.

* * *

Why does this book offer such a complex picture of how Asian Americans fare in the US corporate workplace? Part of the answer comes from the subjects' stories about themselves. This group is even more credentialed, skilled, and personable than any census data show. They earn more than average Asian Americans, hold degrees from highly selective colleges, and have honed their social skills at elite jobs and within select social groups. Many of their parents are highly educated and have consequently transferred social capital to their offspring.

However, some of the people I interviewed explained that despite their background, training, credentials, and social skills, they found it difficult to gain the "trust" of executives at the highest levels. Informal assessments and performance reviews tell them that they need to work on "soft skills." They feel as if they need to stay on a "tightrope" so they don't experience a "backlash" for not performing as expected.

Early on at the midcareer managerial level, this population has difficulty finding mentors and sponsors. They are often ignored or not invited to the table and are not given plum assignments. Taken as a group, these factors increase time between promotions and create leaks in the pipeline to the executive C-suites. This state of affairs is baffling to many of the people I interviewed, given that they attended the very same elite colleges and graduate schools as their colleagues and superiors. "We're not all that different," interviewees said, except for the fact that they are Asian American and their superiors are usually white.

That is the point. At the highest level, race matters more than many people would admit and certainly more than many people acknowledge. Race affects the movement of Asian Americans up the work ladder. Racial discrimination and/or implicit bias are clearly operating, especially at the top levels. Between 2014 and 2016, when I conducted my interviews, some expressed doubt about the success of Asian Americans, and paradoxically many organizations were beginning to be ambivalent about including this group in diversity programs on the grounds that they didn't need such programs, being so credentialed. However, as Gee and Peck note in their 2018 article in *Harvard Business Review*, "If you do not intentionally include, you will unintentionally exclude."

The backgrounds of the people I interviewed confirmed the findings of Lauren Rivera in her 2015 book *Pedigree: How Elite Students Get Elite Jobs*: when it comes to professional jobs, employers prefer to hire prestigious Ivy League graduates. About half of my interviewees have undergraduate and in some cases graduate degrees from Ivy League colleges, along with such prestigious institutions as MIT and Stanford. In these entry-level jobs, the majority earn over a hundred thousand dollars a year.

These attainments place them into a category that I label elite specialized professionals. They can be found in a variety of industries, including finance, media, law, insurance, and creative technology (as opposed to coding). When they describe their difficulties moving up through the ranks, their accounts clarify the nature of a glass ceiling—what many Asian Americans call a bamboo ceiling. Coupled with reports from the business world of the existence of few Asian American executives despite their swelling numbers in entry-level professional pipelines, there is an implication that a barrier prevents Asian Americans from moving ahead in the world of business.

I examine such issues as family background, the institutional characteristics of the colleges they attended, and a wide variety of systemic factors at the workplace—informal and formal programs such as affirmative action, training programs, and mentoring and evaluation processes—that raise issues of assignments, speaking up, soft skills, leadership, and trust.

* * *

Still, efforts to isolate the experiences of second-generation Asian Americans in the work world are few and superficial. Rarely is this population separated from Asian Americans who came to the United States at the age of age thirteen or older. Nevertheless, while research about how the labor market is incorporating second-generation Asian Americans is still marginal, most of the studies that do exist conclude that returns on education and promotions up to management-level jobs are much lower than for their white American counterparts.

For this reason, understanding the mechanisms involved and laying a framework for how individuals move up the promotion ladder, especially past the middle-management level, are vital. Researchers in immigration and organizations need to study what happens to second-generation Asian Americans as they acquire experience and accrue responsibility at work. It is important to determine if and how educational achievement offers benefits when members of these groups enter the corporate labor market.

In chapter 1, I describe the Asian Americans I interviewed—their backgrounds, their hometowns, their parents' occupations, where they went to college, their experiences on the job involving coworkers, and how all these factors may influence if and when they are promoted.

I grouped my respondents into three categories based on which decade—the 1980s, the 1990s, and the 2000s—they graduated from college. Though each cohort has a different relationship to policies like affirmative action and thus has different opinions on how best to move ahead in the workplace, all three of these cohorts are members of today's workplace, with the 1980s cohort the smallest and the 2000s cohort the largest.

The people I interviewed graduated from Ivy League and other prestigious institutions. They work in finance, venture capital, law, technology start-ups, accounting firms, media companies, and nonprofits, among many other fields. The three cohorts I examine have witnessed different trends in American society and have faced a variety of situations in the corporate world. Nonetheless, they share the experience of being among the first Asian Americans to benefit from affirmative action programs and to witness large-scale immigration and growing numbers of Asian Americans in US colleges.

In chapter 2, I discuss a "playbook": a set of maxims forming an ever-shifting collection of oral advice handed down from generation to generation among Asian Americans. This advice, an essential if unspoken element of handed-down precepts for living from one generation to the next, is designed to instruct young people as to the best way to make their way in the world, whether by compiling an impressive academic record or achieving in various extracurricular activities designed to enhance their portfolio when it comes time to apply for college (which it's assumed they'll attend, graduate from, and perform well in). And it is this playbook that in many respects lies at the heart of the dilemmas and challenges that second-generation Asian Americans face when they enter the world of work.

The playbook, of course, is not literal, and its precepts are not written down, but it is pervasive. It also emphasizes the attitudes young people should cultivate—that is, aiming to achieve on one's own, keeping one's head down, working hard, and concealing any failure. It also prescribes the sorts of careers that Asian Americans are expected to pursue—professional work, medicine, and law. They're not expected to pursue careers in the arts, where success is less quantifiable and failure a greater risk. The playbook is practical, instrumental, optimistic, and actually very helpful—up to a point.

While young Asian Americans don't use the term "playbook," it's clear they refer to its precepts when they say, "My parents always told me . . ." or "My friends told me. . . ." It's abundantly clear from my conversations with them that they have been raised to follow these precepts religiously, in terms of both their performance and their attitudes. Finally when one thinks of the model minority, it is likely in part because it's assumed that young Asian Americans will follow the precepts embodied in the play-book to meet the high standard both throughout school and afterward in their work life.

In chapter 3, I examine to what extent parental encouragement, college recruiting programs, compensation, prestige, campus climate, and peers encourage Asian Americans to pursue certain kinds of corporate jobs that offer relatively risk-free employment. However, because for a variety of reasons Asian Americans often move laterally within a company, it frequently takes longer for them to earn the title and compensation they feel they deserve, if they earn them at all. This pattern explains why some Asian Americans may be hobbled from the very beginning of their time in the workplace.

In chapter 4, I explore the work world and how Asian American professionals are climbing the corporate ladder. I examine the forms of capital (social and human) acquired in college and how they are transferable to the various skills needed in the workplace, along with how professionals of different generations navigate routes to promotion and the significance of race and/or ethnicity in these processes.

In chapter 5, I examine the very mixed and often dispiriting experiences of Asian Americans who are at or near the executive level. As members of this group have discovered, the higher they rise, the fewer fellow Asian Americans they find, the result of which is a growing lack of mentors and sponsors. This lack makes it increasingly difficult for this population to move up through a corporation's executive ranks.

In chapter 6, I discuss the unique problems Asian American women confront in the workplace. Like men, they face Asian American stereotypes, and because they are also women, they represent a double minority. They also face questions about their ability to be likable, to lead, to negotiate, to balance work and family, and to respond to sexual harassment.

In the conclusion, I examine the double-edged implications of the "pull yourself up by your bootstraps" mantra that is inferred in the playbook and that is ingrained in the vast majority of second-generation Asian Americans. I also explore why a belief in this mantra can make it hard for young Asian Americans to recognize the critical importance of constricting racial attitudes in the corporate workplace.

As my research and analysis show, the fate of Asian Americans in the corporate workplace is influenced by a complex web of factors, many of which hobble members of this group as they seek to ascend the corporate ladder. Only by recognizing this framework and of course understanding and confronting these factors will their outlook improve.

1

Aspiring Young Asian Americans

ASIAN American professional workers have been hidden in plain sight for over thirty years. They are best positioned to succeed as adults by virtue of their family's social class background, hyperselectivity, and their own academic credentials. They are the offspring of immigrants and are either American-born or members of the so-called 1.5 generation, those Asian Americans who came to the United States with their parents before the age of thirteen.[1] Members of this generation speak English that is indistinguishable from that of other native-born Americans.

Asian Americans are stereotyped as the model minority. Although they are well educated and land jobs in elite fields, they are typically unable to climb to the top of the ladder. By analyzing census data in new ways, complemented by interviews with members of these generations, it is possible to make the argument that many more Asian Americans could have obtained higher-level positions in corporate America.

In this book I broadly describe members of both groups, the native born and generation 1.5, as members of the second generation because collectively they are perceived as being Americanized Asian Americans. All of them spent their formative years being integrated into American society and are US citizens. They grew up in America and attended school in the United States. They were born in the United States or, for those who immigrated, started school in America before the age of thirteen. As we will see, this approach is especially useful when it comes to analyzing the US Census Bureau's American Community Survey (ACS) and Public Use

Microdata Series (PUMS) data. And these data, combined with extensive interviews with group members show that they typically land jobs in elite fields but have great difficulty moving into high-level positions.

As a result of the passage of the Immigration and Nationality Act of 1965 (also known as the Hart-Celler Act), which radically expanded the global pool from which immigrants to America could be drawn, the United States is home to many capable second-generation Asian American adults who in theory should have moved into corporate leadership positions. Some of the oldest members of this generation are well over sixty and stood at the forefront of efforts to enhance civil rights for minorities in this country, notably in the area of greater access to higher education and corporate jobs.

But although census data and reports in the news media tout the successes of this group, statistics show that they are not members of the executive leadership teams of many of the country's best-known corporations. In fact, we know little about how second-generation Asian Americans are faring in the corporate world. An analysis of the experiences of this group in corporate America is long overdue; although there have been some articles published in academic journals, this work represents the first book-length research on this group and how they are faring in this environment.

To explore this issue, between 2014 and 2016 I interviewed 103 Asian Americans with roots in six Asian countries, ranging in age from their late twenties to late fifties. They were from six Asian American ethnic groups: Chinese American, Korean American, Japanese American, Indian American, Vietnamese American, and Pilipino American. They lived on both coasts, in Texas, and in Chicago. I found my first thirty or so interviewees via Ivy League alumni networks and the others through what is known as snowball recruitment.[2] The majority of this group were friends, relatives, or colleagues of the initial interviewees.

I spoke with each subject for at least an hour in person, on the phone, or via Skype. We met in my office at Hunter College, at coffee shops, in restaurants, and in university clubs. I had follow-up interviews or email exchanges with many of them.

My subjects fell in the category of elite specialized professionals in such fields as finance, law, media, insurance, and creative technology. In their careers, the trajectory up the corporate ladder (i.e., becoming a partner or a managing director) is often evident by the time they are in their mid- or late thirties. If we examine full-time professional workers in the for-profit and nonprofit sectors who are between the ages of twenty-five and sixty-four, 40 percent of them are broadly defined as second-generation Asian Americans.[3] Thus there are enough members of this group to begin to understand their lives as adults and how they are faring in corporate America.

History

In 2018 the United States was home to an estimated 22.6 million Asian Americans, including first-generation immigrants, their children, and native-born, who accounted for 6.9 percent of the US population.[4] This represented a significant increase from 1965, when they represented only 1.2 percent of the population.

Today, the entire Asian American group is growing at a faster pace than any other group in the country. It is projected that by 2065 they will represent 14 percent of the nation's population and compose nearly 40 percent of all immigrants entering the country. Immigrants from Asia, an area that includes a total of at least nineteen national origins in East, South, and Southeast Asia, represent a more diverse population than that of Latin American immigrants because there is such a wide range when it comes to income, education, and ethnicity.[5] This group has great income inequality, and this inequality is rising rapidly among and within all Asian ethnic groups. Six ethnic groups made up at least 85 percent of the Asian American population in 2015.[6] Ranked according to their numbers, these groups are Chinese at 4.9 million, Indian at 3.98

million, Filipino at 3.89 million, Vietnamese at 1.9 million, Korean at 1.82 million, and Japanese at 1.4 million.[7]

Immigration

Because of laws that severely restricted immigration of Asians to the United States, the country was home to very few Asian immigrants prior to 1965. For the most part, until 1943 Asians were legally barred from entering the United States through the Chinese Exclusion Act of 1882, which banned the majority of immigration from China. Along with the Immigration Act of 1917 and the National Origins Act of 1924, immigration was banned from all of Asia.

From 1943 to 1965, the number of Asians immigrating to the United States was still very limited thanks to the National Origins Act. Asians began to immigrate in greater numbers only after the passage of the Immigration and Nationality Act of 1965, also known as the Hart-Celler Act, which is the basis for current immigration laws under which family members are given a priority. Those already in the United States wanted to reunite with family members, and those able to support relatives recognized that America offered great opportunities for them and their children.[8] Census data show that in the five decades following passage of the Hart-Celler Act, which was far less restrictive than previous immigration laws, more than twelve million Asians entered the United States.[9]

In 1990, under President George H. W. Bush, the nation's immigration laws were modified yet again, making more slots available for the educated, who were clearly preferred, and limiting those for families' more distant relatives. Unsurprisingly, in 2017 Asian immigrants held more than 80 percent of all H-1B visas, temporary visas that give preference to immigrants possessing special skills needed in the United States, such as those related to the high-tech and health fields, and at one point were cited as creating a "brain drain" from Asian countries.[10] In 2017, 61 percent of Asian Americans, immigrants, and their children aged twenty-five and older held college degrees, compared to 40 percent of

Whites, 30 percent of blacks, and 20 percent of Hispanics.[11] Moreover, over 20 percent of Ivy League students are Asian American.

Census data also reveal that Asian Americans have the nation's highest household income at $73,060, compared to $53,600 for the country as a whole.[12] In addition, three-fourths of all Asian Americans live in ten states, seven of which have a higher overall median income than that of the nation as a whole: New Jersey ($69,829), Hawaii ($65,191), Virginia ($62,173), California ($59,540), Washington ($57,201), New York ($55,712), Illinois ($54,644), Pennsylvania ($50,548), Texas ($50,010), and Florida ($45,609). Since these states have a higher cost of living, residents' median income is higher as well. Coupled with their high levels of education, it is obvious that the national median income of Asian Americans is above national averages.[13] Their high levels of education and greater median income reinforce the impression that Asian Americans are the so-called model minority, performing much better than other groups in the country and doing so by themselves, on their own.[14] One explanation is that many Asian immigrants are hyperselected. Hyperselectivity applies to Asian immigrants who on average are more likely to have a college degree than the nonmigrants from their home country and simultaneously are also more likely to have a college degree than the same ethnic immigrant group in their new country, the United States.[15]

Some of the Asian adults who came to the United States with college degrees in hand have been able to convert those credentials into well-paying jobs. However, many immigrants, lacking education or sufficient fluency in English, could not do this. As a result, they entered such fields as food service, textiles, manufacturing, construction, and small business entrepreneurship.[16] They are members of the working class or the lower middle class who may own a small mom-and-pop business. Behind that high median income Asian Americans are actually the nation's most economically bifurcated group, with the greatest income inequality.[17]

To be sure, some Asian Americans in the working class have a college or other higher education degree from their homeland, but typically they have had trouble converting their learned trade or educational credentials into marketable skills in the United States. Many of these Asian immigrants lacked sufficient fluency in English, or recertifying themselves in the field in which they were trained proved too formidable. For example, some Asian Americans who were trained as doctors had to repeat medical school in order to practice their profession. Understandably, many simply gave up and chose another line of work to survive in their adopted country.[18]

The numbers of foreign-educated adult immigrants contribute to the large number of Asian Americans holding college degrees, and many of their children, both the second generation (those born in the United States) and members of the 1.5 generation (those who came to the United States when they were under thirteen), go on to college.[19] According to census data, regardless of whether the immigrant parents are poor or well-to-do, educated or not, their children seem to be performing well in school. In fact, most studies of second-generation Asian Americans affirm that when it comes to education the American-born and -raised generation is doing exceptionally well in the United States.[20]

These studies underscore the positive narrative that education is the great equalizer, that going to school will provide the greatest opportunities for children of immigrants. It is no wonder that Asian American adults who, like my respondents, are children of immigrants are optimistic about their future even though they themselves may have experienced setbacks and faced discrimination. Their success in education has not translated to attaining positions at the highest levels of their occupations. This conclusion was echoed in a 2019 academic article, "Revisiting the Asian Second-Generation Advantage," written by sociologist Van Tran from the CUNY Graduate Center, sociologist Jennifer Lee, and graduate student Tiffany Huang from Columbia University. Using census data, the authors found lower returns from education for second-generation adults. Data from the 2016 National Asian American Survey also support the finding that Asian Americans perceive higher levels of discrimination due to race in comparison to native-born whites and native-born Latinos.[21]

The Second Generation

Most sociological studies of Asian Americans have focused on the young children of immigrants still in school and disregarded the adult second generation in the work world because the latter group seems fewer in number. In addition, studies of Asian Americans in the workplace fail to differentiate between those raised in Asia and those raised in America. Criticism of studies that show the slow advancement of Asian Americans up the corporate ladder is often answered with the refrain of "give it more time" or "there aren't enough American-born or American-raised yet" to enter those ranks. These findings are usually based on census data compiled after 1965, which indicate only whether a person is a foreign-born or native-born American. Using data without differentiating between these two groups, foreign-born immigrants who came as adults and foreign-born immigrants who came as children before the age of thirteen (the 1.5 generation), will result in "miscounts."[22]

However, as I illustrate in this chapter, using census counts and the US Census Bureau's American Community Survey (ACS), data regarding the second generation, defined as American-born and -raised, enough people fall into this category to help us understand what happens when they try to advance in corporate America. With help from the Center for Urban Research at the Graduate Center/CUNY I have been able to analyze census PUMS and ACS data so as to include members of the 1.5 generation.[23]

Let me describe some of the weaknesses in the vast majority of studies that do not account for the 1.5 generation. It is very easy to underestimate the number of Asian Americans born and raised in the United States and to discount their experiences. The Census Bureau and its ACS differentiate only between the native-born and the foreign-born. Their calculations fail to reflect how we socially define Asian Americans who do not have an accent, were raised in the United States, and attended American schools throughout their teenage years. For most of the 1.5 generation, the United States is the only country they have known. Although these young people are socially Americanized and are citizens, they are included among the foreign-born in the census. And for this reason, to best understand how Asian Americans are faring in America's corporate workplace, it is necessary to examine the experiences of not only the native-born generation but also the 1.5 generation because both spent a considerable portion of their early years in America and both are largely the product of the American school system.

In examining the number of Asian Americans working full-time in the private and nonprofit sectors, the data from the PUMS 2013–17 ACS combined five-year file show that among Asian Americans between the ages of twenty-five and sixty-four, 59.9 percent are foreign-born and 40.1 percent are second-generation (native-born plus generation 1.5) Asian Americans (see Figure A.1). For women, the ratio is approximately the same. There are 59 percent foreign-born and 41 percent second-generation (native-born plus 1.5 generation) Asian American women in the employed database (see Table A.1).

In fact, the size of the second generation has steadily increased since the Hart-Celler Act was passed in 1965. The second-generation children of the earliest immigrants after 1965 would now be at least fifty years old. Each succeeding decade brought more immigrants, along with their children. Among immigrants who didn't bring children with them, many had children in the United States. For all these reasons, the Asian American population rose from a low of 1.2 percent of the US population in 1965 to 6.9 percent as of 2018.

Over the decades Asian Americans have had various relationships to affirmative action, diversity, and other programs designed to address discrimination and to aid them in education and the workplace. Thus to understand the second generation in depth, I have divided them into three groups, based on when they graduated from college.

For this study I interviewed Asian Americans who graduated from college in the 1980s, 1990s, and 2000s. Large numbers of Asian Americans began entering elite colleges in the 1980s after the civil rights movement opened doors for them. Many colleges, especially elite institutions such as Harvard, implemented race-based affirmative action programs that included Asian Americans. Along with African Americans and Latinos, Asian Americans became the first group of people of color who achieved critical mass on college campuses. Tufts sociologist Natasha Warikoo, in her 2016 *The Diversity Bargain: And Other Dilemmas of Race, Admissions, and Meritocracy at Elite Universities*, explains the latest incarnation of affirmative action and how it is tied to diversity.[24]

Many colleges still have race-based programs that include Asian Americans. However, the perceptions of these programs have changed over the years, as have the perceptions of whom they benefit. In addition, depending on whether they entered the work world in the 1980s or the aughts, Asian Americans were confronted with various mixes of ethnic groups in the workplace and varying access to training programs and the ability to pursue specific careers.

I've divided up Asian American twenty-five- to sixty-four-year-olds into four age cohorts (see Table A.2 for more information). The oldest cohort comprises roughly the group who graduated in the 1980s along with some who graduated in the 1970s, who represent the youngest of the baby boomers and some members of Generation X. The forty-five- to fifty-four-year-olds are mostly members of Generation X and graduated college in the 1990s. The thirty-five- to forty-four-year-olds and the twenty-five- to thirty-four-year-olds are mostly members of Generation Y or millennials and graduated from college in the 2000s. These, of course, are just approximate groupings with blurring at the edges, just as affirmative action and diversity policies likely to affect this population in corporations and in private and public education also have fluid boundaries.

Using ACS 2013–17 data on population trends, within just the private and nonprofit sectors one can examine age cohorts of second-generation Asian Americans. As can be seen in Table A.2, the younger cohorts clearly include a significantly higher proportion of young people who are second-generation Asian Americans. For example, 42.5 percent of all second-generation Chinese Americans fall in the twenty-five to thirty-four age group, as compared to only 8.9 percent in the fifty-five to sixty-four group. But for the second generation as a whole, 31.5 percent fall into the thirty-five to forty-four range, which is the group that should be making significant strides in ascending professional ladders.

It's not surprising that my sample had so few second-generation South Asian Americans, most of whom are actually still quite young. There are far fewer of them to interview than there are second-generation Chinese and Korean Americans (see Table A.3, which gives the proportion of the second generation by ethnic group, and Figure A.1). Of all ethnic groups, the largest divide between foreign-born and second-generation is among Asian Indians and South Asians. Of Asian Indian American thirty-five- to forty-four-year-olds, 82 percent were foreign-born, with only 18 percent part of the second generation, with similar numbers for South Asian Americans as a whole. For another example, 54 percent of Korean Americans in the thirty-five to forty-four range are second generation, versus 46 percent foreign-born. This explains why plenty second-generation Korean Americans volunteered for this study.

The Interviewees

Given the structure of professional work and the promotional ladders in such fields as law, banking, consulting, insurance, and creative technology, where most of the people I interviewed are employed, many workers reach management levels within ten to fifteen years of beginning their career. In theory, many of the respondents should be able to make partner, managing director, or vice president by their late thirties or early forties, if they get their job right out of college or graduate school. Thus it is important to see who makes up the thirty-five to forty-four cohort. Table A.3 indicates that a significant number of Asian Americans, about 42 percent of the thirty-five to forty-four group, were second generation (broadly defined native-born and generation 1.5) and could have reached this threshold.

To understand the professional trajectories of this population, it is useful to separate individuals in terms of the year they graduated from college. The ten-year markers for age used by the ACS clarify the underlying population changes and how important it is to examine the newly revealed second-generation adult Asian American population. When it comes to understanding how members of this population moved ahead in their careers, each cohort tells a different and important story. Between 1980 and 2016 each individual as well as each ethnic or racial group—Asian Americans as well as African Americans, Latinos, and women—experienced different degrees of receptiveness from formerly white-shoe corporations via systems that kept some members of these groups isolated while a few others flourished.

Between 2014 and 2016 I interviewed 103 Asian American professionals aged twenty-eight to fifty-seven and members of this second generation, which, as I have mentioned, includes the 1.5 generation, focusing on their progress in the workplace. The other main criteria for participating in my study included that the individuals had graduated from college sometime between the 1980s and the 2000s, were not employed as backroom technicians, and were evaluated with performance reviews.

Over these years I came to know some of the subjects personally, and many in turn connected me with their friends. I did field work and attended panel discussions, meetings, and conferences. All this revealed a professional work world that is far more diverse than the one I remember when I graduated from Harvard in 1984 and started working at IBM. Yet this world is still deeply stratified by gender, race, and class—not surprisingly, despite decades of affirmative action programs. At the very top, in the corner offices, there are still few women and few people of color to be found.

The CEOs of *Fortune* 500 companies are overwhelmingly white males. Fewer than a dozen CEOs in the *Fortune* 500 are Asian; three are black and twenty-four are women.[25] Even though Asian Americans are seen as the model minority, they occupy few of those offices. Although well educated and thus well represented at the lower levels of their professions, they are not climbing the professional ladder into upper-echelon positions. Not only are white males the majority of the CEOs, but they also remain the highest paid.[26]

The ten-year span for each cohort allowed me to see significant differences in approaches used and resources available for each group. All of those interviewed earned upward of ninety-five thousand dollars a year, and many earned much more, well above the national median income for Asian Americans (the ethnic and educational backgrounds of interviewees are summarized in Tables A.4 and A.5).

The Asian American Elite

The participants clearly form an elite group with a fairly elite background. In his 2011 book *Privilege: The Making of an Adolescent Elite at St. Paul's School*, Shamus Khan, professor of sociology at Columbia University, explained why groups can be elite and how, at least with education, some groups can have some mobility. Those who hold power and have control of and access to resources and institutions are generally considered elite. Khan explains that Asian Americans, the children of fairly successful parents, themselves also educated, can be considered elite because of their income, which has become a determining factor in light of growing income inequality.

Asian Americans possess a certain amount of economic clout. In 2017 they had the highest median household income of all racial groups, at $81,331 a year.[27] While this number is high, the spread is great. The lowest median household income ($39,730) was for the Burmese, the highest ($114,261) for Asian Indians. This large gap also indicates that Asian Americans have the greatest income inequality of all racial groups.[28] The people I interviewed are clearly members of the income elite.

A second criterion to determine who is a member of the elite is the institutions they are affiliated with. Most of the people I interviewed attended prestigious colleges or worked for well-known firms in corporate

America. (The colleges they attended are listed in Table A.5.) There is no doubt that the right socialization and influential peers help too. As Lauren Rivera, a sociologist at the Kellogg School of Management at Northwestern University, wrote in her 2015 book *Pedigree*, students from elite colleges are often recruited and hired by elite firms. These firms believe that these colleges help to vet the students for them. While her sample included very few Asian Americans—only two of thirty-two— her overall findings with regard to elite firms hiring graduates of elite schools ring true.

Some of the elite firms represented in my sample include Goldman Sachs, BlackRock, TIAA-CREF (now known as TIAA), Citibank, the Federal Bank of New York, HBO, MTV, Time Warner, and many other smaller and less well-known but highly competitive firms. The job titles my interviewees held included development officer, partner, director, global program manager, chief operating officer, general manager, managing director, and senior vice president.

Those interviewed were mostly ethnic Chinese Americans, the largest Asian ethnic group in the United States. The majority of interviewees also attended institutions ranked as "selective" or "most selective" by such publications as *USA Today*. This may be related to the fact that most of their immigrant parents hold college degrees and are more educated than many of the native-born parents of similar ethnic groups. They have been able to make use of their educational credentials in the United States, thereby accessing the resources necessary to send their children to better schools and colleges from which these companies recruit their employees.[29]

In theory, the children of the working class can also join these professions. Earlier studies by Kasinitz et al., Louie, and Lee and Zhou indicate that working-class children do just as well as their better-off peers in school, even with fewer similar resources, although the adult children of working-class parents may lack the networks that can be transferred only by wealthier and more educated parents.[30] I had few respondents from working-class backgrounds in these job categories, so it seems to me that members of this working-class group may have chosen to enter professions that require more technical skills as a safeguard against discrimination.[31] They would rather be doctors, lab technicians, pharmacists, and computer scientists than high-level executives at major companies.

The people I interviewed overwhelmingly live either on the East Coast (predominantly in the Mid-Atlantic states and the Northeast) or on the West Coast (California and Oregon); some lived in Texas or Chicago. About half of them are married, and a quarter of those marriages are interracial unions. Many of the married couples have third- or even fourth-generation Asian American children, and some have mixed-race children. Some of the people I interviewed grew up in cities, a few in Chinatowns, but the majority were raised in suburbs where there were few other Asian Americans.

None of this is surprising given that the majority of their parents have college degrees and are members of the middle class who were able to move anywhere in the nation to find work. They graduated from some of the best colleges in the United States (Table A.5) and work for some of the nation's wealthiest and most important companies. They earn at least ninety-five thousand dollars annually, and most of them earn well over that amount.

The Parents: The First Generation

The parents of the people I interviewed are employed and solidly middle class. They are engineers, doctors, nurses, professors, real estate brokers, carpenters, security guards, garment workers, small-business owners, dry cleaners, grocery store owners, and restaurant operators. They work in cities and suburbs. This was somewhat of a surprise because in general there ought to be more working-class parents among this group because there are many native-born Asian Americans who are children of the working class. I suspect that the children of working-class parents are in different professions than the group I chose to examine. Perhaps they are working in STEM fields that are considered more economically secure.

Surprisingly, nearly 75 percent of the Asian Americans I interviewed had at least one parent with a college degree (see Table A.6). Only about half of the parents of the oldest cohort had a college degree, whereas over 80 percent of the youngest cohort had at least one college-educated parent. Thus this particular group is especially advantaged, and yet as will be discussed in the last chapter, only seven (or 7 percent of my total interviewees) of them have made it to leadership teams. When studying the elite in general, parental class and educational status play roles in helping define or propel a group into powerful positions. Surprisingly, parents' education and class standing may not confer a higher status to their adult American-born and -raised children because it may be mitigated by their race or parents' immigrant status or access to social networks.

Child Rearing

Not surprisingly, some of the parents of these high-achieving young Asian Americans could be classified as so-called tiger parents of the kind that Amy Chua, a professor at Yale Law School, described in her 2011 best seller, *Battle Hymn of the Tiger Mother*. Such parents are extraordinarily strict when it comes to setting exceptionally high bars for performance within and outside of the classroom. Chua's approach, although viewed as extreme and even punitive in many quarters, is a twisted reflection of what is known as the immigrant bargain parable— often invoked by first-generation parents. This narrative depicts immigrant parents as leaving everything behind in their homelands to immigrate to the United States so as to forge a better life for their children. Their children's success is repayment for their parents' sacrifices. Chua, who is a second-generation Asian American parent, born in Illinois, invokes the narrative in a slightly distorted way as her children just owe repayment to her for all the work she has put into tiger parenting her third-generation children.

The research is based on the children fulfilling the terms of this pact so as to justify the hardships their immigrant parents endured. Thus, pressure on the second generation to achieve is tremendous. Many scholars, including sociology professors Cynthia Feliciano, Tomás Jiménez, Jennifer Lee, Vivian Louie, Robert Smith, Van Tran, and Min Zhou, have written about parents who use this narrative to constantly remind their children to work hard so as to pay back their parents for making such huge sacrifices. The argument is that these children owe their parents and can repay their debt by getting a good education, preferably at an Ivy League college, and embarking on a successful career. Although not all Asian American parents invoke the immigrant bargain, the idea of leaving one's country and giving up everything for the sake of one's offspring is a major tenet of the playbook, a verbal advice checklist on how to succeed for Asian Americans that will be discussed in depth in chapter 2.

As a consequence, in many competitions involving science, spelling, robotics, music, dance, and athletics, a growing number of Asian Americans are winning laurels. Some of the people I interviewed, like the proverbial tiger cubs, excelled in violin, piano, and schoolwork. Others resembled the children described in "What Asian Americans Really Care about When They Care about Education," an article by Amherst sociologist Pawan Dhingra that was published in 2018 in the *Sociological Quarterly*. Their parents typically do as much as they can to keep their children competitive in this world in which it is increasingly difficult to gain acceptance to Ivy League schools, and thus presumably to acquire greater social mobility. As a consequence, some children enter virtually any competition that their parents insist on. For example, Dhingra discusses how competitions like spelling bees allow Asian American children to compete in a field other than athletics, an area in which South Asian immigrant parents are typically more proficient as coaches.

Still other parents believe that emulating their peers is a surefire way to success. They tell their children to look at children a bit older to see how they obtained great grades, recommendations, and records in extracurricular activities and to emulate them. In other words, parents tell their children to act like their peers.[32] In fact, the playbook spells out the specific activities that children should participate in to be successful. In other words, the playbook lists tried-and-true approaches that have worked in the past.

A few respondents had parents who encouraged them to participate in activities that help the family—for example, earning money to help support the household or caring for younger siblings. In these households, family responsibilities came first. And finally, to the surprise of many young Asian Americans, some Asian American parents simply let their children pursue any activities they wanted to, regardless of the dictates of the playbook.

Parents and Discrimination

For the most part, the respondents did not report specifics about discrimination that their parents may have encountered. These parents avoided discussing their experiences in detail because they believed that their offspring, as children of immigrants, would not face discrimination because they were US citizens, either born or raised in America, and because they spoke perfect English. However, in reviewing the responses of the people I interviewed, I found that their parents experienced discrimination regardless of whether or not they held college and graduate degrees or were working class and regardless of the age of the respondent.[33] In other words, discrimination occurred not too long ago, although many of the respondents of varying ages told me that explicit discrimination that their parents faced was a thing of the past.

One of the 1980s college graduates described how disappointed her father was in the 1970s when he couldn't get a mortgage to buy a house in several neighborhoods in Brooklyn. Apparently he had tried a number of times, but no bank would loan him money. Only later did her mother explain that the mortgage was denied because of a policy known as redlining and that it was designed to keep Asian Americans, along with other minorities, from buying houses in certain neighborhoods. At the time the respondent didn't think much of the incident, but now she realizes that her father was denied the money because of racism.

Another respondent described in detail the discrimination her father faced when he tried to build a hotel in the Southwest after settling the family in Texas in the mid 1990s. "We opened the motel in 1995," she recalled. "It was a brand-new construction. It was hard because at the same time my mom and brother and sister and I, we were still in Dallas, and my dad he was driving back and forth because he had to oversee construction. It was just one of the many instances when he felt race was a big deal because he saw the construction guys, they were all Anglo-American, and I think they saw dad, and they were like, oh, this inexperienced man, who didn't know English. . . . The project that should have only taken eight months to complete drags out to fifteen months," she continued. "So because it was dragging long, my dad ended up making the decision to leave the family in Dallas and literally drive a minivan to Phoenix. He lived out of his car for the remaining six, seven months because he had to supervise these guys and make sure they were actually doing the work."

Even though the parents of my respondents were overwhelmingly college educated, they learned English as a second language and spoke with an accent. This is an area in which the respondents reported incidents involving their parents that were frustrating or could be seen as examples of discrimination or explicit bias. The parents were often ignored, purposely misunderstood, or even made fun of for their accents.[34] Most of their parents believed that their status as immigrants and lack of English skills held them back in work and other areas, and thus they believed that their children, proficient in English, would suffer no consequences on this front.[35] However, the responses of the people I interviewed showed that biased attitudes even with their second-generation status and ability to speak perfect English could be linked directly to their race as Asian Americans. And here there is a disconnect, showing how much race still matters, even for the American children of immigrants.

The 1980s College Graduates

The 1980s college graduates were among the first recognizable members of a cohort to enter corporate America. But while growing up, they were immersed in everyday American life and also experiencing the aftermath of the civil rights movement. As children they were among the group that benefitted from the movement and the desegregation policies that resulted. They were too young to march but watched from the sidelines. The oldest US-born members of this group entered kindergarten in 1963, nearly a decade after the US Supreme Court ruled that school segregation was unconstitutional (although before the 1971 Supreme Court ruling that upheld the use of busing to achieve school segregation). Some of them acknowledged that they were bused to school as part of desegregation efforts, received awards that included them as underrepresented minorities, and benefited from affirmative action programs in higher education and the workplace, which began to go into effect in the 1960s.

The worldview of the 1980s college graduates was shaped by the historic and demographic forces at work in the United States during the time they were growing up. These included the optimism of their own families and the openness of institutions that included Asian Americans in affirmative action programs. They were the new minority on the block. Not only were they not seen as undesirable, but they were regarded by many as a positive influence; it was believed that they could indeed work harder and become the model minority. Because of this perception, some of the respondents did not think that any racism was directed toward them.

About half of the members of this group remembered particular racist episodes that shaped their outlook on race in America. The majority remember their parents' experience with discrimination. Some remember not only their parents' inability to obtain mortgages in better neighborhoods but also their parents' inability to get better professional jobs. Many remember being bullied or made fun of as children. They remember being called names like Ching Chong and being teased about the strange food they ate, the shape of their eyes, the sound of the language their parents spoke, and in general the foreignness of their nationality.

Their numbers were small, and they were included in many college recruitment and support programs that already included African Americans and Latinos. Even though they graduated from college during Ronald Reagan's presidency, a politically conservative era in American history, institutional policies such as affirmative action were still in effect for African Americans, Latinos, Native Americans, and Asian Americans. Many of the 1980s college graduates were also among the first few Asian Americans from their high school to attend an Ivy League college or be recruited by prestigious boarding schools and private day schools.

Thus by their thirties members of this group remained optimistic and satisfied with their own successes because they saw progress and had little else to compare it to. At that time few Asian Americans held leadership positions in American corporations. However, as second-generation sons and daughters, they followed a professional track as expected.

Typical of this group is Chinese American Fred, a 1982 Stanford graduate and holder of a Harvard MBA, currently a finance executive. A California native, he remembers that as a child during the 1970s he was bussed from his overwhelmingly Chinese neighborhood to a school in a predominantly black neighborhood. He remembers his working-class parents protesting the decision along with other Chinese immigrants. His parents even kept him out of school for a while. But in the end they relented and he was bussed to middle school.

Fred noted that being Asian American brought its own complications, especially in a world that he thought was only black or white. But he also remembered being considered for a financial award that normally went to an African American or Latino student. And through college and into the working world, he was always considered for special programs to help him advance. As he described the awards, I was struck by the fact that he never labeled them as coming from organizations that sought him out for affirmative action or diversity awards, even though I knew that this helped explain why he was chosen for such honors.

That was in the 1970s and 1980s. By the time Fred reached midcareer in the late 1990s and early 2000s, that was no longer the case. As he recalled, he was promoted based on his analytic, technical, and product knowledge and how well he worked with other members of his team. Fred, who is in an interracial marriage and has two grown children, believed that he helped opened the doors for many Asian Americans who followed him. In fact, he feels that he should mentor many more Asian Americans as "obviously they still need it." Like many of his peers, he mentioned that his employees noticed him mostly because of his intelligence and smarts, but he felt limited because he had also been encouraged to improve his social skills, especially if he wanted to be in leadership.

For many Asian Americans of this generation, a key event occurred in 1982, when Vincent Chin, a twenty-seven-year-old Chinese American who lived in Michigan, died after a severe beating by two laid-off auto-workers who accused him of being Japanese and thus responsible for their being unemployed at a time when Japanese automakers were competing with the Americans. Rickie, a Chinese American and a 1987 Yale graduate, recalled that she was deeply shaken by this widely publicized murder. She recalled reading that the murderers got only a "slap on the wrist" for the vicious attack. She was shocked, she said, never thinking that such a thing could happen to an Asian American.

Like Fred, Rickie became much more aware of her identity as an Asian American. She also realized that she was one of the few Asian Americans to attend a top school and work for a finance firm. But unlike Fred, she recognized that Asian Americans could ascend only so far. While working on the trading floor of the New York Stock Exchange, she saw the almost exclusively white boys' club in action. She subsequently worked in Asia, believing that working abroad would be the surest way to be promoted. Her performance reviews encouraged her to learn new skills; in fact, she was given what was described as "the chance to excel" through a year working in the firm's Hong Kong branch.

When Rickie returned to the United States, she was promoted as had been promised. However, working overseas seemed to pigeonhole her as an "Asia expert" when she simply wanted to be known as someone who took risks by working in Asia at a moment when China was still just opening up its markets to the rest of the world. Rickie did not speak Chinese and had never been in Asia until her placement there.

Much to her dismay, her quick ascent in the firm slowed down after that experience. Even though the company was well meaning, she was completely stereotyped after that experience. By promoting her strength in her ethnic community, some instead saw her as clannish. As was the case with Vincent Chin, her colleagues also saw her as a foreigner.

When members of this cohort were in college and joining the workforce, they felt as if they were paving the way both for themselves and for those who came after them. As one interviewee put it, he thought that he was "clearing the path for everyone to follow." Wherever they went, they stood out as the only or one of the very few Asian Americans, a token in a classroom or in their departments at work.

While they were optimistic, they also felt that they had to "represent"—to stand for all Asian Americans—by doing the best they could because each shouldered the responsibility of having to do well so that every Asian American following them would have the same opportunities that they themselves had. Their parents reinforced the importance of not bringing shame or failure to their families or to the larger Asian American community.[36] By the time they reached midcareer jobs, most agreed that they had done very well and were pleasantly surprised by how important a position they had ascended to in their corporations.

They and their parents remained optimistic because very few Asian Americans had forged the road ahead of them and thus they had little with which to compare their accomplishments. They were essentially the pioneers. Of course there was room for improvement for those following them, but at least this prediction came true for all the people I interviewed who graduated in the 1980s. They were all better off than their parents in terms of income, education, and work status. A larger number of this cohort were first-generation college students, so the social and professional distance between them and their parents was particularly significant. Moreover, they reported that outright racism did not worsen over the more than thirty years in their careers, although the form of discrimination had changed to less outright racism and more implicit bias.

A 1989 graduate noted that by the time he graduated from college, only twenty-five years had elapsed since the sweeping Civil Rights Act of 1964 had been passed: "There have been tremendous changes ending segregation." Nevertheless, by the time members of this group reached college, most of them still realized that they were not part of the mainstream. There had been plenty of progress, but they were still not fully accepted. They were the ones pushing the envelope.

Today, more than thirty years after their own college graduation, a majority of them couldn't help but wonder why things had moved so slowly for the cohorts following them. They believed that there should be more Asian Americans at the helm, given that they were able to move relatively quickly up through the ranks at the corporations where they were working, and given the fact that many more Asian Americans attended elite colleges after them, and that data show that they have the nation's highest median incomes and have attained the highest levels of education.

These oldest interviewees spoke less than the younger ones about having a clear path to follow, even though they also mentioned the double-edged model minority myth. They did not credit their success to their Asian culture. Instead, they spoke of following a trial-and-error path while they were trying to fulfill their parents' implicit and sometimes explicit immigrant bargain—to do better for their parents since they had given up so much to come to the United States.

Indeed, the oldest Asian American interviewees included by far the greatest number of members of the working class and were definitely the ones clearing the path for younger Asian Americans. Moreover, this older cohort noticed that the parents of the 1990s graduates and the

1990s graduates themselves were much more knowledgeable than they had been about the process of getting into college and landing a job. This was partly due to their increased social capital and their ability to use coethnic resources and tips or information from the 1980s graduates.

The 1990s College Graduates

The 1990s college graduates are a more diverse group. The immigration stream that produced them is extremely varied because their parents came from ethnic and socioeconomic backgrounds that were very different from one another. Some parents are currently professionals and engineers, while others were educated abroad but could not transfer their credentials after they emigrated, thus having to work in blue-collar jobs. Still others are solidly members of the working class and have had little formal education.

These second-generation Asian Americans had access to the experiences of the 1980s graduates in myriad ways. Many of the 1990s graduates attended the same high schools, lived in the same communities, and even attended the same churches and mosques as Asian Americans from the older cohorts.

These families were also more diverse. The more wealthy and educated immigrant parents mixed with the working-class parents who had come to the United States in earlier decades. Some of the immigrant parents who had arrived more recently and who could not convert their college degrees to the American equivalents or did not speak English became entrepreneurs or other professionals in the local ethnic communities. The working-class and the more highly educated and resource-rich immigrants pooled their talents to create ethnic community organizations that supported the next decades of Asian American students. Min Zhou wrote about these ethnic resources as early as 1992 in her book *Chinatown: The Socioeconomic Potential of an Urban Enclave* and again in her 2009 article.[37]

The newly created services offered in the communities were afford-able and widely available to both working-class and wealthier second-generation Asian American children.[38] Offerings included Asian language classes, supplemental or enriched coursework, test prep classes, and opportunities for extracurricular activities and leadership in Asian cultural arts and community service, all of which helped when members of this group were applying to college.[39] These activities proved to be an excellent way to fulfill some of the requirements spelled out in the playbook.

The 1990s graduates were extremely interested in networking and supplemented their friendships with 1980s graduates with member-ship in many professional organizations, such as the National Associa-tion of Asian American Professionals (NAAAP). Their interest helped these organizations grow during the 1990s; the NAAAP, for example, which became a national organization in 1991, had begun in the 1980s with only three chapters. With the help of these associations and men-torships, many Asian Americans moved up career ladders during the 1990s, although very few occupied executive suites. Nevertheless, the 1990s graduates sought to follow a playbook whose tenets had been es-tablished by more experienced Asian Americans.

The worldview of the 1990s graduates is complex. Members of this group were unusually confident, as they had many more resources from their wealthy parents, greater access to established community cen-ters, and the help of Asian American mentors, frequently 1980s college graduates, who shared their own experiences of getting into college and landing a job. I was surprised to learn that while the 1980s graduates (most of whom came from working-class families) sought practical jobs in such fields as accounting, some of the 1990s graduates reported that they were told by their parents that finance was an unacceptable career choice because back then it did not require a graduate degree. Hyein Lee and I write about this particular group in our 2015–16 paper, "Navi-gating the Road to Work: Second-Generation Asian American Finance

Workers." This attitude, they reported, was a remnant of Confucian beliefs, which stressed academic accomplishment or a practical career and denigrated work in finance on the grounds that it did not contribute to public welfare. Thus, those 1990s graduates who wanted to be doctors, engineers, or lawyers received the blessings of their parents. However, I believe there is a class or status dimension in the choice of professions. For some Asian American parents of the 1990 graduates, it is much more impressive to say a child has become a doctor, engineer, or lawyer.[40]

Some of my respondents explained that as their numbers in higher education increased, their success was due to their parental and community resources and cultural heritage. Some did not believe in nor mention affirmative action programs. Some said that policies such as affirmative action would have no consequences when it came to college admissions and entry and rise in the workplace. Others, however, did mention affirmative programs that had helped them achieve success. Their varied responses echoed debates around California's Proposition 209, which in 1996 widely prohibited discrimination on the basis of race, sex, and ethnicity.[41]

The 1990s was a time of considerable debate about dismantling affirmative action and instead supporting color-blind policies. In 1989 Harvard was investigated by the Office of Civil Rights of the US Department of Education about whether the university discriminated against Asian Americans.[42] Although Harvard was found not guilty, the conversation had clearly shifted from the 1980s, and the decade witnessed an increased number of attacks on affirmative action. As a result, affirmative action became a way to increase diversity on campus and in the workplace and less of a restorative justice program. Nevertheless, if the playbook included listings of race-based programs that could help Asian Americans, some members of this group made use of them.

Overall, the 1990s graduates did well. They closely followed the advice of the 1980s graduates and did exactly what their parents suggested. Both sets of advice were also in the playbook.

Typical of this group was Mie, who was raised in the 1980s by Japanese expatriate parents and graduated from college in the 1990s. Mie moved quickly up the ladder in a large multinational consulting firm and became a senior vice president by midcareer. At the time I interviewed her, she had decided that she wanted to step off the corporate treadmill and become a full-time parent before returning to the workplace.

Mie, who was born in Japan, arrived in the United States when she was six years old. She already knew English and speaks without an accent; her father was also fluent in English. She lived in Forest Hills, Queens, attended elementary and middle school there, went to a specialized high school, and then attended a highly selective college. She was accustomed to talking with executives from her father's firm and watching her mother entertain "American style." She also played tennis well.

Mie had a very sophisticated understanding of race relations in the United States. She noted that both whites and African Americans saw Asians and Asian Americans as threats. In particular, she noted that Americans of all races had lost jobs to Japanese manufacturers and thus scapegoated Asian Americans (like many Asian Americans, she was familiar with the story of Vincent Chin).

Mie also knew that African Americans felt cheated when Korean Americans opened mom-and-pop grocery stores in black neighborhoods ahead of them, a conflict that was explored powerfully in the 1989 Spike Lee movie *Do the Right Thing*. She also cited the three days of rioting in Los Angeles that followed the 1992 acquittal of police officers for the beating of African American Rodney King, when black looters destroyed countless stores owned by Koreans. She felt that she had many advantages over African Americans but did not have the same advantages as white Americans. However, she explained, she saw herself not in the middle of a white-black hierarchy but rather standing on parallel tracks, able to move forward in certain areas like education but not in others like entertainment.

The 2000s College Graduates

The 2000s graduates were only in their late twenties and mid-thirties when I interviewed them. The most important historical events for them were the terrorist attacks of September 11, 2001, and the recession beginning in 2007. Like other college graduates, they had trouble finding jobs after those two events and after being laid off. As Marlene Kim of the Economic Policy Institute concluded in a 2012 report, Asian Americans had the highest share of unemployed workers and were typically unemployed for more than six months, far longer than people from any other group. This conclusion was supported by several of my respondents.[43]

Very few of them could recall the boycotts of the Korean-owned stores or the tension between Asian American store owners and their African American customers, especially in New York and Los Angeles. However, they do remember their parents' experiences. Having just left their parents' household, they have fresh memories of their parents' experiences. Many of them have seen their immigrant parents hit glass ceilings in engineering jobs. A few also witnessed their parents being laid off after either September 11 or the great recession. One respondent was laid off at the same time as her father; they strategized to look for work together.

This younger group also experienced an increase in discrimination or bias against older immigrants like their parents. Wen Ho Lee, a Taiwanese American scientist who was detained on what turned out to be false espionage charges, was mentioned by several of the people I interviewed.[44] His 2002 autobiography, *My Country versus Me*, chronicled how his civil rights were taken away partly because the US government stereotyped him as a foreigner stealing secrets for China. In the opinion of the people I interviewed, the case only reinforced the notion that even after so many years in the United States, Asian Americans were still viewed as foreigners. As the sociologist Mia Tuan described them in the title of her 1998 book, *Forever Foreigners or Honorary Whites?*

By 2000 Asian Americans represented 3.6 percent of the US population and some communities were beginning to notice a marked increase in Asian American families.[45] As the sociologists Tomás Jiménez and Adam Horowitz concluded in their 2013 article, "When White Is Just Alright: How Immigrants Redefine Achievement and Reconfigure the Ethnoracial Hierarchy," Asian American students are doing so well academically that even white students use Asian Americans as the standard to compete against. This state of affairs, the authors note, alters the assimilation process because now a person can aspire to be like a member of a nonwhite group. But in other communities, where whites compete with Asian Americans for limited spots in a school system, there is plenty of resentment against the high academic achievement of Asian Americans. Working hard for high grades and high SAT scores, using test prep services, and attending extra classes, Asian Americans were often viewed as unfair competition.

The 2000s also brought another view of affirmative action, and opponents of the practice are still bringing lawsuits against institutions that make use of it. Two cases brought against the University of Michigan and argued in the US Supreme Court in 2003 (*Gratz v. Bollinger* and *Grutter v. Bollinger*) upheld the use of race as one of many factors when selecting students. Meanwhile, through local court arguments and ballot initiatives, states rolled back the use of race.[46]

The narrative shifted once again where beneficiaries of affirmative action found themselves ashamed or defensive. If race was used as a factor when it came to college admission, it was easy for them to conclude that they therefore weren't worthy or deserving of that college seat. This assumption was clearly upsetting for all students who benefited from affirmative action but especially so for Asian Americans, who believed that their hard work, as reflected in their test scores, made them worthy and deserving. In response, supporters of affirmative action reminded Asian Americans that college admission was based on a multitude of factors including test scores, extracurricular activities, personal essays, and more. Race was just one factor.

Typical of this population is Edmund, a Chinese American 2002 graduate of Stonybrook, part of the State University of New York, a public institution. Edmund, who lived in Sunset Park, Brooklyn, had a difficult time finding a job in marketing. He looked for a job during his entire senior year, with no luck. By the time September 2002 rolled around, he began applying to local graduate programs in social science research to enhance his research skills. He was subsequently accepted by New York University, Columbia, Queens College, and Hunter College, but without the scholarship he needed. In the end he started his graduate program at Hunter College in the fall of 2003 and found a full-time job after a year.

Edmund said he enjoys his job in marketing but feels he has had to insist on working with customers. He has noticed that there are few Asian Americans in his area. He did not want to be relegated to crunching numbers in a back room, and though he had many job interviews prior to accepting this job, he felt that he was the victim of implicit bias and stereotyping, especially of people like him who, in the opinion of managers, lacked social skills and didn't want to work directly with people.

One experience—basically a bait and switch—left an especially bad impression. Edmund came to be interviewed for a job that included working with customers but was told that the opening was for a back-room marketing support position. After the interview he politely declined the offer. Such stereotyping, he believes, discourages people from seeking jobs in sales and marketing. Moreover, he said, "It was obvious that there were no diversity programs for Asian Americans here."

As the portraits of these Asian Americans show, every positive image is typically connected to a negative image. To be smart is to lack social skills, as Fred discussed. Working with coethnics can be seen as cliquey or clannish, as in the case of Rickie. To work hard is to compete unfairly, as shown in the Jiménez and Horowitz study.

The number of adult second-generation Asian Americans is significant and will continue to grow. But while they remain very positive in their outlook, they realize that simply increasing their numbers in the workplace will not automatically help them ascend to higher levels in corporate America. While attitudes toward Asian Americans in the workplace have evolved and in many ways improved over the last several decades, achieving equality remains an elusive goal, and even programs like affirmative action (because they have been cut or have been watered down) have not gone far enough.

2

The Playbook for Success

My mother told me that if I wanted to go to Harvard, I needed to do the same activities as the Asian American kid who got into Harvard the year before. So on top of good scores and grades, I needed to be first violin in the school orchestra, and I needed to be a captain of my swim team. And I did, and I got into Harvard.

—Vince, a Chinese American who graduated from college in the 1990s and is now a partner in a law firm

WHILE the United States was home to many fewer Asian Americans in the years before 1965, my analysis begins with the older cohort of pioneering second-generation Asian Americans who graduated from college in the late 1960s and early 1970s.[1] These Asian Americans were among the small group of nonwhite students entering mainly white institutions just as the gains of the civil rights movement were crystallizing. Their experiences in college and in the workplace, where they were also trailblazers, helped establish the larger context for understanding the successive waves of second-generation Asian American college graduates and the challenges they faced in corporate America.

Some of these people were eventually promoted to deputy, vice, partner, or chief jobs, in some cases positions that led them to the corner executive office. However, members of the generations that came after them had difficulty replicating their success. There are a number of reasons, as we shall see.

First, there are few Asian Americans at that high level who can share information about how the corporate workplace functions. Second, most of the information that is shared is about how to "pull yourselves up by your own bootstraps," and there is only so much control people can have over their own destiny when there is still both overt and implicit bias.[2] Third, there has been a push-back against company efforts to bring more Asian Americans into higher education and the workplace, specifically against affirmative action and diversity programs designed to help them get a foothold in elite colleges and later elite jobs. Today there are fewer efforts and fewer Asian Americans willing to admit that they were once participants in them. An unspoken false assumption is that people who use these programs to gain access are unworthy because they didn't do it on their own. The playbook is a significant part of the overall framework contributing to the difficult time that Asian Americans have in moving up corporate ladders.

A second-generation Chinese American male who graduated in the late 1960s offered one explanation. Watching today's second-generation Asian Americans who are about twenty years younger than him and in the middle of their careers, he said, "It's like a bad TV rerun playing in prime time. . . . When I was working in the 1970s, we confronted racism. We would say it's going to be better for my kids. But guess what? We're still discussing similar issues." He added, "Those at the top like to promote those who look like themselves," who are white and male.

Another Asian American I interviewed, a late 1990s graduate, acknowledged that he was not at all surprised that few Asian Americans held leadership positions in corporate America. In fact, he is trying to teach his teenage third-generation children that the world is not fair, that it is "not a meritocracy" where rewards are based on one's ability. He doesn't want them to hold on to the stereotypes and racism used against Asian Americans, both of which can have very real negative effects. He would rather have them build self-confidence and see the positive aspects of their own images. However, he also wants them to understand how the world operates and be realistic about barriers they may face. "Sports is the analogy I use," he said. "The coach has favorites; there are certain plays that rely only on certain people. Certain players will get more play time or time to execute plays better. The crowd has favorites. The work world has favorites, too."

Still another interviewee contended that Asian Americans can move up in the corporate workplace, but only with many people helping. "You can't do what you did in school, like being nice and always pleasing your coworkers and managers," he said. "Hard work alone doesn't cut it. There were few people who I could ask to help, but I finally figured it out. You need a lot of reinforcement from your supporters. It took me a long time to figure out how to get that reinforcement to make sure that my voice and ideas are heard. The advice for Asian Americans at this level is vague because so few have made it."

These observations make it clear that Asian Americans have varying beliefs and explanations as to why more of them cannot be found in corporate executive suites. All these comments make sense. But there is one story that is told again and again, a story that drowns out these explanations that speak to structural aspects of the American workplace: there are too few Asian Americans who can share information, and structural programs that help have decreased. The dominant narrative among Asian Americans is that they must and will *make it on their own*. They must work hard, doubly hard. Yet at the same time the bulk of Asian Americans also have a whole set of values, behaviors, and stereotypes ascribed to them that can hurt as well as help them ascend job ladders, as we have seen.

However, according to the optimism reflected in these views, nothing is inevitable. What young people starting out don't know, they can learn. And if they aren't promoted up the hierarchy, they can try other ways to compensate for their deficiencies, including taking part in leadership training such as the Stanford Asian American Executive Program, enrolling in public speaking courses such as Toastmasters, hiring executive coaches, and enrolling in other programs designed to change their behavior and appearance and help them stand out and be noticed.

It is this self-reliance, the belief that one can control one's destiny, that can both propel and limit. There is nothing wrong with self-help and knowing that one has the capacity to improve. However, recognizing that

Asian Americans, like African Americans or Latinos or women, have many things in common and then asking to be included in institutional diversity programs or reaching out to potential mentors or sponsors are also necessary skills if a person hopes to move up the ladder. Even though teamwork, helping others, building trust, and, most importantly, asking for help are some of the key levers involved in moving up, most Asian Americans, when figuring out how to ascend the corporate ladder, still view themselves as self-made individuals, using individual effort without acknowledging that a person must also know how and when to ask for advice and support or to change the systemic processes. And of course Asian Americans are not the only ones who hold this philosophy.

The Playbook and the Ideal of the Self-Made Asian American

One way to understanding this behavior is to analyze the Asian American "playbook." I have coined this term to label an almost universally used guide composed of verbal advice that Asian Americans use as they move through school and into the professional world. For the most part, my subjects and their Asian American parents know its contents—some of which I have described above. Regardless of how young Asian Americans behave during a job interview or a similar situation—and there are plenty of deviations to the prescriptions in the playbook—almost all of the respondents will share the general playbook narrative and then tell me how much they followed or deviated from it.

The playbook is a verbally transmitted, informal, and practical "how-to" guide for Asian Americans designed to show them how to "make it" and be successful at both school and work. These tips are passed on to help young Asian Americans attain the ideal of the Asian American dream, where Asian Americans are part of a multiethnic society that is open to people of all backgrounds. In this scenario, story, or narrative, Asian Americans work hard, have access to opportunity, are able to be in control of situations, choose what they want to do with their lives, and find rewards for themselves and their families. I believe that mine is the first book to describe this "Asian American guide" and how it is used in the workplace, despite its extensive use in Asian American families.

This guide dovetails with the achievement-minded Asian American image or frame that the mainstream American public accepts as the generic story of Asian Americans.[3] It also reflects the aspirations that all immigrants have. Immigrants are generally optimistic and believe that their children will do better in their new homeland.[4] In addition, not only will the children do better, but they have an obligation to do better.

As the sociologists Jennifer Lee and Min Zhou wrote in their 2015 book *Asian American Achievement Paradox* and as Vivian Louie, a sociologist and director of the Asian American Studies Center and Program at Hunter College, wrote in her 2012 book *Keeping the Immigrant Bargain: The Costs and Rewards of Success in America*, the playbook has been important for parents because the goal is for the generation born and raised in America to be successful because their immigrant parents sacrificed so much for their offspring. Often, the parents left behind a much better life in order to provide a better future for their children. In response, the second generation must do its best to fulfill this immigrant bargain, and the tips in the playbook help them to achieve this too.[5] These two powerful books mention narratives that are similar to those my respondents told. Thus they keep the narrative of the playbook circulating among Asian Americans. Moreover, these two books, along with playbook scenarios generated by relatively successful Asian Americans, who often leave out times when they failed, are persuasive enough to lull many into believing that the majority of Asian Americans are doing well in the American workplace. Thus, anyone who can't do as well as the image suggests is almost shamed into silence.[6] For all these reasons, the advice, tips, and stories contained in the playbook become the dominant narrative.

The critical role of the playbook was the single most common narrative among the individuals I interviewed. Elements in the playbook were often mentioned at many research-related professional events I attended, including meetings and conferences hosted by pan–Asian American and diversity professional organizations. Thus these impressions from the playbook on how to be successful are reinforced over and over.

Origins of the Playbook (Part 1)

Outsiders may think the tips in the playbook are really just Asian culture transplanted to the United States, especially since many believe that Asians are education- and status-minded. However, the ideas in the playbook are specific to American institutions. Asian immigrant parents figured out how to adapt to institutions in the United States. Earlier immigrants and their children catalogued successful efforts to earn good wages in specific fields (e.g., science, technology, engineering, and math—STEM), learned by experience that a college degree granted social mobility, and determined which high schools and colleges allowed easier access to those jobs. Once these parents learned generally about social mobility, they used their resources to create approaches and programs (creating test prep centers, programs for extracurricular activities, job coaching programs) to help their American children make their way into these American high schools, colleges, and jobs.[7]

The advice was shortened to tips and curated based on actual lived experiences and outcomes of the Asian American second generation who have had success in the workplace. As reported by nearly all of the people I interviewed, the main elements of the playbook are the "goals," "scripts," "checklists," sets of "rules," and "tips" as well as a catalogue of resources that a person should access to be successful in life.

The playbook is highly practical. Asian Americans in my sample are narrowly focused on following the prescriptions in the playbook, the goal being to live the American dream. The advice is couched in a way to encourage each person to work hard on his or her own to follow the playbook. However, according to many interviewees and statements made at conferences, there is a lack of information on why these tips may work and why others are not included. Most notably absent from the playbook is a historical, political, or legal context to explain how second-generation Asian Americans have fared in schools and the work world.

Origins of the Playbook (Part 2)

Asian immigrants raising children in the United States face many challenges, including language difficulties. Some have lower-paying jobs. Some Asian and Asian Americans have received lower returns than white Americans despite having reached the same educational levels, and struggled more in some of those jobs.[8] Even Asian immigrants who are well educated often find themselves stepping into unexplored terrain, especially when it comes to getting their children into certain schools and later helping them enter the work world.[9]

Even immigrant parents who work in corporations or professions may lack the social connections and ability necessary to move with ease and confidence among their mostly white American coworkers. They may also be relegated to the back offices of corporations and thus not have access to information on what is necessary to occupy the front office. Many of my respondents' immigrant parents were engineers or scientists, but whether educated or not, poor or wealthy, parents often find the American education system and the culture of corporate professional work unfamiliar.

However, my research shows that the playbook is not specifically tailored to helping a person move up the occupational hierarchy much past the midcareer level. A corporation does not operate like a school or college, especially in terms of how individuals proceed up the career ladder. A corporation generally has its own business model or professional culture that defines the qualities necessary in the people management wants to promote.[10] Typically they are looking for candidates who can lead employees on lower rungs of the ladder and collaborate with supervisors on the higher rungs.

Corporations have their own rules, created usually by those in leadership and passed down by each successive wave of leadership, which are often opaque to subordinates. Complicating matters, Asian Americans typically have limited access to the top echelons of the corporate world. They are so thinly represented in those ranks that sharing information on how to ascend to those levels is inadequate and often nonexistent.[11]

The prescriptions in the playbook are based on what has worked for Asian Americans who were successful at least to the midcareer level. Many of these maxims are extensions of advice that worked in school and college: complete each assignment the best you can, score the highest number of points possible on exams, become a leader, listen to teachers, be cooperative with classmates, work hard, stay out of trouble, speak up only when necessary, keep your head down at school, make friends. Of course these are still reasonable and helpful, and in fact some are indispensable behaviors, but they are not enough to guarantee a person's success in the world of work.[12]

The playbook has another drawback: it doesn't always detail the processes that allow these transformations. Become a leader—but how do you become a leader, and what does it mean to be a leader in the work world? Make friends—but how do you treat work colleagues? The playbook doesn't explain that moving up at work doesn't just mean executing a perfect project or presentation (like getting perfect scores in school) but means being assigned the plum assignments or getting opportunities to excel so as to get one's name recognized by one's superiors and to thicken one's personnel file for performance reviews.

As one of the people I interviewed put it, "You can do the best in any project, but to get recognition, especially promotion points, you need to work on a high-profile assignment that is significant to higher-level management." *Which* projects a person does well on sometimes matters more than simply doing well on any project. The playbook offers no advice on how to land this kind of high-profile assignment. And predictably the playbook approaches the world of work the same way it approaches the world of education.[13] It's not surprising that this is true, especially since lofty test scores, good grades, and a raft of extracurricular activities and internships often help students get into a college and land a job.

Not surprisingly, Asian American parents, community leaders, and peers share playbook recommendations or narratives to encourage the second generation to do well. Asian American college graduates over the past four decades share revised and updated versions of the playbook when they meet with other Asian American high school or college students and alumni in classes, at social clubs, and as part of career activities. Asian American business groups share these suggestions too. And of course they are shared among other corporate workers and in professional organizations. Some people I interviewed even noted that the playbook narrative is shared among non–Asian Americans.

Nevertheless, its concepts are taught primarily to Asian Americans (young and old) in the ethnic community, in organizations such as after-school programs for elementary-school-aged children, at test prep programs for preteens and teenagers, and to entire families in religious institutions like mosques, churches, and temples.[14]

Individuals who want to follow a path and adhere to it precisely follow its maxims carefully. The contents of the playbook are noncontroversial and always practical and include very little advice about handling discrimination or disappointment,[15] even though native-born Asian Americans regardless of gender perceived more discrimination than whites and Hispanics when it came to winning promotions.[16] Perhaps, as some of the respondents said, it is because some who share the precepts of the playbook would rather just dismiss the idea of discrimination in the work world than tackle it, or just make a joke and laugh it off instead of bringing up racism and race, an uncomfortable subject for many. Many of my interviewees say they address it this way because they see discrimination as microaggressions between individuals—themselves and the other. They don't place these incidents in a structural framework. Asian American professional workers are instructed to keep their heads down and told that if they work hard they will be noticed.[17]

As a fiftysomething South Asian American stated in an open forum on diversity at the workplace, the goal is to "get a degree and do well in one of the Asian immigrant parent-approved jobs, that is, be a doctor, lawyer, engineer, scientist . . . or be a loser." While this comment was laughed off, the people I interviewed recognized its sincerity, given the advice they received from their own immigrant parents—and the playbook.

According to the people I interviewed, the playbook strongly approves of master's and doctorate degrees and of STEM careers. Asian immigrant parents believe that the degrees and the skills acquired in these areas, once acquired, cannot be taken away from their offspring. Moreover, these fields and higher degrees lead to jobs that the parents perceive to be less discriminatory in both the short run and the long run.

How the Playbook Spread

The playbook became widespread in the 1980s as more Asian Americans came of age and the demand for guidance became insatiable. Newspapers, television, and community groups (later through digital media) reported how young people moved up the mobility ladder and reported on Asian Americans who won all kinds of academic awards. Many young Asian Americans wanted to follow those who were able to move up.[18] While others were more wary,[19] parents and young adults of all Asian backgrounds shared the ideas in the playbook to grasp and master the mechanisms necessary to help young people move into professional jobs.[20] Many members of the Asian American second generation, especially those who graduated from college in the 1990s and 2000s, followed this guide devotedly, whether they lived in New York City or Kansas City.

The playbook is everywhere because it transcends class, ethnicity, gender, and even age. Many Asian Americans, especially those who are like my respondents with college-educated parents, have in their head a version of a list of prescriptions, a rulebook, a road map. Many Asian Americans follow the route outlined in the playbook through school and into the work world. After forty years, the playbook recommendations have expanded, but they are still well known in immigrant Asian American communities. They are still shared across generations and among peers, and especially passed along from mentors to the young people they advise.

Specifics of the Asian American Playbook

As one of my interviewees put it, "Every time I was in a Korean setting, I was told to just defer to authority, to my elders, shut up, work hard, don't ask questions, don't be confrontational, and if you do that, good things will happen. That worked up to a certain point. So keeping your head down, working really hard, going to public schools that were really focusing on grades, testing. I graduated with a great GPA. I went to MIT undergrad, graduated MIT with a good GPA, then got a job at a finance firm."

"I was an analyst," he added. "I branded myself as someone who is extremely hard working, trustworthy, really good with numbers, I could build models in my sleep. If you want something to get done, you give it to Eric.

"And then I got promoted to associate. Same thing. Managing directors and partners would fight to have me on their team because they knew I would get shit done. I got great bonuses. So it was all good. Then I got promoted to VP. And then at VP my first performance review wasn't great because they said I didn't speak up enough and that I wasn't 'commercial' enough." This proved deeply upsetting; the analyst had thought he was following the playbook to the letter.[21]

Typical too were the comments of a young woman from Chicago who is in her thirties, graduated from college in 2000, and holds an MBA. She told me that her parents, both of whom were from Taiwan, spelled out for her a certain set of rules that she had to follow if she wanted to achieve success. Some items were specific; for example, if she wanted to get into a good college, along with earning top grades she had to become editor in chief of her school newspaper and learn to play the piano. She had to have academic, leadership, and musical skills, all at the highest level possible. At college she majored in a science because that was the subject area where she could excel with less discrimination. The underlying message was that she had to work extra hard in every area. While she no longer felt pressured to make her parents happy, she was still attuned to working hard because doing so helped her succeed.

A similar story was told by a 1990s MBA graduate of the University of California, Berkeley, who is now a vice president in the finance industry. He was, he said, "brought up the Taiwanese way, meaning never good enough until we're the best. How wrong is that?" He also said that part of the drill was to assimilate, to be a member of the tennis team, to be a leader.

Even people who acknowledged that their parents were similar to tiger parents, those who expected only the very best from their children, share similar sentiments as those in the playbook. Immigrant parents, some of whom can be characterized as tiger parents, would actually be stricter when following playbook tenets. Their own versions of the playbook would place even more emphasis on achievement, performance, and more prestigious activities. Tiger parents would ensure that their children follow the rules in the playbook by disciplining them strictly because for tiger parents to succeed was not enough; their children had to be the best at everything. And frequently, as my respondents also mentioned, tiger parents would also compare their children's performance with those of the other kids in their social circle. And a couple mentioned that this type of parenting made it seem as though their parents' love was conditional. Thus the pressure and demands on these tiger cubs were even greater than those on the offspring of non-tiger parents.

Some of their other Asian American friends faced similar demands; although they were admonished if they didn't get straight As or didn't follow all the rules, they didn't have to be number one. What stuck for this population was that the rules embodied in the playbook still ring true. The playbook worked for many in the Asian American community and continues to do so.

More important, even though some young Asian Americans felt obligated to follow those rules, they also learned that using individual effort could really improve their performance, that practice really does help. This led many to believe in self-empowerment, a belief that they could control the steps necessary for success. And of course extending that notion, they believed that if they followed the prescriptions in the playbook they would be able to ascend the career ladder.

The Playbook at School

The playbook clearly anticipates that members of the second generation will earn top grades in elementary and high school, be obedient, excel in extracurricular activities, and win competitions. Teachers of Asian American children encourage students to compete in academic activities, and most parents support such competition. For example, teachers advise many Asian Americans to participate in the Intel (Regeneron as of 2016) Science Talent Search, play a classical musical instrument, join an orchestra, join an athletic team in sports like badminton, volleyball, swimming, or soccer, or join an academic team and compete in math olympiads, spelling bees, and quiz and history bowls.[22] Their chances of acceptance to a prestigious college would increase with participation in these activities. The parents know this too.

"But so, yeah, and I think up until the end of college it was sort of like, hey, if you work hard and you buckle down and you were kind of the best at what you did, everything was just fine. And that's pretty much how our parents are raised; you go to the right school, which where they are from it's SKY—Seoul National, Korea University, or Yongsei, that's pretty much it. There are lots of colleges, but if you go to one of those three you pretty much rule the country and get any job you want. Unfortunately that's not how it works in the US."

Most of those interviewed said their parents had "high expectations" and set a "high bar of excellence" for them. Immigrant parents want their children to get accepted by Ivy League colleges like Harvard, Princeton, or Yale or a prestigious school like Stanford.[23] Likewise, at college these Asian Americans generally understand how to do well in school. It's about studying and getting honors and doing some activities that you enjoy, but it's mostly about getting the degree. Finally, as seniors in college, some capitalized on summer internships to convert them to full-time jobs or used career centers and job fairs to search for a professional job. Still others prepared for graduate school.

As a fortysomething Chinese American woman who holds a bachelor's degree and an MBA from Harvard told me, "Growing up Asian American is a blessing and a curse. I didn't have to insert in my own thinking. Even in my first job, an apprentice-type job, just being an Asian American good girl made me my bosses' favorite. Work hard, be deferential."

The Playbook for Midlevel Professionals

Once in the work world, second-generation Asian Americans followed a parallel set of rules that members of the 1980s cohort say was sometimes improvised, sometimes quite haphazardly. The 1990s cohort found the playbook quite useful. The 2000s cohort had a few more older alumni to connect with if they had problems. But on the whole they relied on the contours of the playbook they had used for school. They had lots of practice working hard, being compliant and respectful, and acquiring technical skills, the very same skills that got them high marks and good recommendations in high school and college. They work long hours, do as directed, try to cooperate and to build connections. When their performance reviews are lackluster, they work even harder.

My respondents tried to figure out what they needed to do as they moved up, but they were not always able to ascertain the requirements for the next level. As was noted by a late fifties Chinese American marketing senior vice president and general manager who became a professional executive coach, having the ability to move up in your first few years means "learning specialized knowledge to be able to do your defined job." That is, he added, if it is "marketing, learning how to put together a plan, knowing where and how to get answers, collecting and using data from your customers." Many of my respondents complained that they spent too many years in entry-level jobs before moving up to midlevel positions.

Another Chinese American respondent, who holds a bachelor's degree from the State University of New York and a master's in business from Fordham, told me that with all Asian Americans, you "don't want to stand out in a crowd, don't want to get anything wrong and be embarrassed," as the playbook puts it. Thus, he continued, "I took fewer risks, and only when I was really frustrated and held back did I turn down projects and started to pick and choose assignments. I was quiet and didn't want to upset the boat for the longest time. I just became disgruntled when I figured out I wasn't in the inner circle and that I wasn't going to get promoted. So I became a slacker, and only did what I needed to. I got to know my coworkers better, and surprisingly, by working less hard, I was promoted." To be clear, he still worked many hours a week, but he spent less time perfecting presentations and graphs.

Like this man, by midlevel in their careers, many people I interviewed had developed professional and personal networks and leadership skills. However, the dynamics and mechanisms that allowed him to get promoted are not spelled out in detail in the playbook.

To be sure, some of the people I interviewed did not have problems reaching middle-management positions, although many thought it took them longer than it did their non–Asian American colleagues. Those who found it easier to reach middle management said that they learned many necessary work skills at college and in summer jobs, primarily gaining polish and earning trust, two important traits required for moving to the next level.

The Playbook Beyond Midlevel Jobs

The people I interviewed agreed that the playbook failed to help them move to the highest levels of the corporate world. Regardless of whether their parents were working class or middle class, the playbook instilled in them the immigrant story of their parents coming to the United States for their benefit. The importance of working hard still rang true.

While the playbook is a guide, it is also a resource to help second-generation Asian Americans round out their skills. The lessons in the playbook are about self-improvement. It doesn't address everything that Asian Americans are missing and what they need to learn to move up in the corporate world. The respondents understand the need to be authentic, to assert themselves, to network, and to engage with their coworkers and, as the executive respondents mentioned, the need to trust team members.

However, some members of the second generation are beginning to think that the playbook is holding them back since its advice is not detailed or nuanced enough to aid the second generation. Some corporate leaders expect Asian Americans to be Eastern, "foreign-born" quiet, consensus-building workers who are content to work hard; others expect the second generation to lead as necessary and step up and assert themselves, especially when there is a vacuum. The advice in the playbook neither addresses these types of leadership skills nor explains how to shift from one to another when appropriate. The playbook also doesn't instruct them on how to shift the structures in the organization to consider different kinds of leadership styles or to provide more specific programs to develop talent in Asian Americans.

Moving Up to the C-suites

Advice on how to move into the highest echelons of corporate America is even more vague. According to the people I interviewed, one explanation for this is that very few second-generation Asian Americans occupy those positions, and among this small group, few are able to share information about ascending to the top.[24] For example, in 2012 just five of the twenty Asian American CEOs of *Fortune* 500 companies had been born in the United States; eight had been born in India, one in Sri Lanka, and one in Pakistan. And these numbers have only gotten worse, as in 2017 there were fewer than a dozen Asian American CEOs of *Fortune* 500 companies, it is not clear how many are Asian or Asian American.[25]

In addition, corporations may have their own strategy for promoting people, a strategy that is opaque to the people I interviewed. Those who have ascended close to that level emphasize that they got to their position by working hard, getting to know their peers, and letting their peers get to know them. They stress the importance of being a self-made person, of pulling themselves up by their own bootstraps. Only if they are extremely self-reflective and candid do they see that they are similar to their peers in terms of such things as education, social interests, and their children's interests. Whether or not they acknowledge it, the world at the top is occupied by people who are more similar than dissimilar across a range of personal qualities and interests. It's possible to move up without these qualities. However, if one doesn't have these qualities, it is difficult to acquire access to the upper echelons without institutional support.

The playbook cites just a few diversity programs, which are newer forms of affirmative action programs. These programs directly recognize the presence of minorities, including Asian Americans, in the workplace. Respondents who went to work in the three decades that were included in this study had access to these programs, some as early as high school. Others were recruited along with other minorities, and some joined these programs while at work.

Respondents connected with these programs moved up faster and higher than many others. These programs offered help that was otherwise not easily attainable. One of these programs, known as Sponsors for Educational Opportunity Scholars, which provided academic course review and SAT prep, and later mentoring was described by some of the interviewees as amazing and was credited with helping some be accepted into first-class undergraduate and internship programs. Respondents who are associated with this program continue to have links to it.

In the late 1990s and early 2000s minority-focused internships and executive training programs became more limited in scope and started to exclude Asian Americans because leaders of corporations saw how many Asian Americans were already in entry-level jobs. However, today corporate diversity programs are being revived because they are beginning to recognize that the numbers of minority executives have stagnated. People I interviewed described these programs as essential for building networks, getting training, and being exposed to different departments of a company and to the company's high-level executives. Lacking such corporate programs, some of my respondents turn to professional groups and executive training programs (sometimes focusing on Asian Americans) that offer mentoring and advice on public speaking. Some hire personal career coaches.

They find other resources to shore up their leadership abilities. They speak to coworkers and seek help from professional organizations like ASCEND Pan-Asian Professional Organization, Leadership Education for Asian Pacifics, Asian Women in Business, the Asian American Bar Association of New York, and the National Association of Asian American Professionals.

They read advice books and articles by executive coach Jane Hyun, including *Breaking the Bamboo Ceiling: Career Strategies for Asians*, published in 2005, and her 2012 article "Leadership Principles for Capitalizing on Culturally Diverse Teams: The Bamboo Ceiling Revisited." They try to learn specific social skills that they think may help and to learn how to convert Eastern-style leadership skills into abilities valued in the West. However, many of them conclude that improved social and people skills are not enough. Many of them are already curious, friendly, and sociable—all characteristics that make for a good coworker but not necessarily a good executive.[26]

At the executive level, one respondent told me, Asian Americans need to learn how to build trust. The playbook offers very little information on that subject. How do the highest-level workers convert their networking and social and human capital into trust, which is seen as necessary to move to a C-suite office? The higher one goes, one person said, the more responsibility one has to help keep the company afloat. At this point, at least metaphorically, a person gets a key to the corporation but can get that key only if the person is trusted.

The Invisible Corporate Playbook

Asian Americans know it is difficult to climb to the top of the corporate ladder. When the pyramid narrows and they see few people who look like them at the top, they know such an ascent is problematic. What surprises many of them is not that they can't reach those peaks but that what they did for so long—that is, following the maxims of the playbook—does not translate into having more Asian Americans in top corporate positions. These respondents always thought that they had more control of their lives than they really did. If they worked hard, if they fixed the things that were wrong, they would be able to move ahead. Or so they thought. Fewer understood that moving ahead was often out of their control.

Some of the people I interviewed who did hit the glass or bamboo ceiling reverted back to the playbook. They doubled down on their efforts to work harder and to use ethnic or professional organizations to reinforce their public speaking skills, improve their leadership skills, and make use of networking, mentors, sponsors, and executive coaches. The respondents focused mostly on interior rather than exterior matters because the overriding narrative in the playbook is that of the self-made person. Again and again, many simply tried to work harder.

Outside of the playbook, they also tried to learn skills necessary to build trust. They tried to be curious about their coworkers, friendly to everyone. But these particular skills are not described in the playbook.

So how does one learn them? Some respondents noted that they learned them in college, observing what they described as the "best schmoozers on campus." Other advice? They practiced. They made an effort to be comfortable among all their friends. They didn't rush to go back to finish a project. They took time at lunch to speak to coworkers. They remembered everyone's name and the activities they liked and their spouses' and children's names. They learned to build trust by sharing more about themselves and asked others to share about themselves. When they had to network at cocktail hours, they made a goal of speaking to at least three individuals and learning about their interests. All these activities helped them become visible to their coworkers, which in the end might also help them get a promotion.

Trust and the Key

Another crucial issue is whether the workplace is willing to meet the worker halfway. Asian Americans have proved that they can learn, but will they be promoted? A few respondents suggested that despite their skills and achievements, the workplace may not be ready to promote them. A few others noted that the workplace must make an effort to include and promote Asian Americans, making more use of diversity, inclusion, and affirmative action programs.

Only a few of the people I interviewed said they would rewrite the playbook to include lessons about pointing out discrimination at work instead of encouraging workers to simply dismiss bias and work harder. Many admitted that if they are treated unfairly, they just brush it off; otherwise they can become labeled as troublemakers and top executives will trust them less. None of the respondents were surprised to learn that they had to network and build their social skill set. They said they had to work smarter by creating their own brand and putting into practice advice from human resources workers, coaching professionals, and mentors. Most respondents said that they would rather "work harder on fixing themselves than question the organization."

Efforts by the Corporations

My interviewees who have made it to the C-suites did not get there via any single route; most of them used a combination of techniques. Quite a few who moved up the ladder in the late 1980s and 1990s credited affirmative action and diversity programs that had explicitly identified minorities for management development. Resources were invested in these programs because the corporations involved saw the value of diverse leadership.

Significantly, participants in these programs learned what was required to be a leader and found themselves in a supportive situation. Periodically, they were assigned to work with executives and given mentors. Among the skills one of my interviewees learned in his affirmation action program was effective networking and building trust. "I'm very conscious of speaking to executives," he said. "For every single person, I try to remember something about them that I can relate to. I need to find that fact and figure out how it relates to me because I have a different background. It's one of the most important skills I learned." He realized that a person had to pursue some self-improvement, but acknowledged that diversity and affirmative action programs offered training and access to higher management to those lucky enough to be in such programs.

One issue is that since young Asian Americans are so shaped by the playbook and the "made it by myself" narrative, they do not want to acknowledge that they were recruited to be in a diversity program. Some of them feel the stigma of such programs. Some of the people I interviewed said they did not want to be associated with such programs because to do so may give the impression that they weren't really qualified for the job. In fact, one person said he initially thought that he was a "failure" when he was tapped for a diversity program, although he later concluded that joining the program was one of the best things he had ever done to advance his career.

A few of my respondents thought there was outright discrimination in the workplace. Some of the people I interviewed said that the workplace is characterized by having some implicit bias. Most agreed that there was very little outright racism or discrimination. An example of indirect bias toward women, for example, is that Asian American women are assumed to be younger than they actually are and thus are not ready for promotion. Another example is that both Asian American men and women are assumed to be lacking leadership skills when in reality they may simply lead in different ways than white managers. This unquestionably affects who gets promoted.

Caveats to the Playbook

Many Asian Americans learn quite abruptly that they need to perform differently than the playbook guidelines to move up in corporate America. However, they tread a fine line between expectations described in the playbook (expectations also shared by teachers, parents, and even many non–Asian American executives) and how they themselves feel they should act. A few suffered from severe backlash from managers and peers if they spoke up or veered too far from expectations as to how Asian Americans are expected to behave in the workplace.[27]

Thus there are discrepancies between the playbook rules and some of the respondents' experiences. But my respondents were uncomfortable acknowledging these discrepancies. Their experiences tell a story that belies the perfect Asian American dream success story. They are reframing the Asian American dream, but their message is getting through only to people who are open to this alternative narrative. This narrative, although more accurate, is messier and unquestionably includes experiences of discrimination. Since success is often characterized as something attainable by oneself, discrimination is also seen as a person's own fault. Thus some Asian Americans feel shame when they can't make it on their own, especially if they have followed the prescriptions in the playbook to the letter.

The Playbook for the Third Generation

Almost all the respondents who are parents of the third generation are willing to stand up to racial bias. They expressed an urgency when it comes to addressing discrimination and want corporations to acknowledge and correct the situation. If they as the American-born or -raised do not stand up at the workplace for their third-generation Asian American children, they ask themselves, who will? Among the group who sees discrimination, they may disagree on the solution, but they are willing to step forward. In fact, their remarks reflect the sentiments of the few 1970s graduates I interviewed, who said, in effect, "Why is it taking so long? There has to be a better way to stop this cycle."

The narrative of the playbook will not be the narrative of their children's lives. Of the respondents who have third-generation children, some are already college graduates. Elite second-generation Asian Americans don't require the playbook the way their parents did. Even if they themselves have hit the bamboo ceiling, they still have more access to resources for their children than their parents ever did. Their friendship circles and their own mentors and sponsors can provide much more information. They can afford to send their children to some of the best schools in the country and live in some of the most expensive neighborhoods. At the same time, they and their children are still on the receiving end of discrimination, both explicit and implicit. But they, unlike their parents, are willing to speak out and actively urge change.

As for parenting, they see that there are myriad ways that their children can grow. There is no strict need for them to attend a certain college or pursue a specific career. A high-level Chinese American executive mother and her Korean American physician husband told me that they are not raising their children the way they were raised. Their children do not, the woman said, "owe us anything, yet we have high expectations. We don't discipline them like the way we were. We're not immigrants. We love them unconditionally, and it's okay that life has its failures."

3

Landing a Job

So one of the VPs that I happened to know in my internship.
connected me to a VP at US Trust. So I was the only Asian American in my immediate group and my immediate group had fifteen people, but then I also worked as biz analyst—I interfaced
between the business sides, also the IT side. And of course the
IT side, you know, 60, 70 percent were Asian American.

—Chinese American female 1990s college graduate

As we have seen, one reason that the challenge of finding a first
job for the broadly defined second-generation Asian American
has not been studied is because it has been widely assumed that members of this group have always been able to find a job, based on their
stereotypical image as a model minority with high educational attainment and incomes, at least when it comes to the corporate world. It's
been assumed that the jobs they find are on a par with those held by
their white counterparts. It has also been assumed that the experiences
of a small native-born group representing just 25 percent of the total
employed Asian Americans aged twenty-five to sixty-four are irrelevant
since members of this group have only recently come to represent a large
proportion of the corporate world. However, when the 1.5 generation
and the native-born are combined to create the broadly defined second
generation, they make up 40 percent of the employed population aged
twenty-five to sixty-four.[1]

Because this group has not been studied, we know little of this process.
What are the push-pull factors affecting young Asian Americans as they
consider various career paths? What are the differences among graduates of Ivy League and other colleges in this regard?[2] And what about

the role that employers play in determining which part of a company an employee is assigned to, regardless of the employee's preferences?

Examining the barriers that are often labeled as the glass ceiling or the bamboo ceiling solely at midcareer overlooks processes that occur much earlier and assumes that Asian Americans follow certain inevitable work patterns. This assumption, in turn, often helps affirm the stereotype that Asian Americans belong only in certain jobs. For example, why is it that Asian Americans are overrepresented, particularly in entry-level positions, in industries such as technology and other quantitative-based fields such as finance and insurance? Why are so many Asian Americans to be found in backroom support-type jobs usually made up of administration and support, rather than client-facing jobs in which the worker interacts with other people?

Hyein Lee and I, in our 2015–16 article, "Navigating the Road to Work: Second-Generation Asian American Finance Workers," found that when it comes to being hired for a first job, the playbook notion that young people are able to do it by themselves simply by working hard has an important place in the minds of young Asian Americans, even if they have access to considerable institutional support. I wrote an article in the sociological journal *Contexts* in 2016, "Asian Americans, Bamboo Ceilings, and Affirmative Action," in which I argued that support is welcome in light of the fact that immigrant parents, even those who have college degrees and earn higher incomes, have few connections to people in the corporate or professional world who can help their children get jobs in these sectors. Moreover, few younger people I interviewed had their own connections to people at a high enough level to help them get a job.

Second-generation Asian Americans work hard to find a first job, making use of such resources as campus employment offices, career fairs, and sometimes their own social connections. But though they hustle and work very hard, professional and corporate human resources departments that do the hiring have their own logic in recruitment, placing more onsite recruiters at the more elite schools and then sorting individuals who apply for jobs in terms of whether they seem to belong in back, middle, or front offices, each with a different ladder to promotion and to the C-suite. Ultimately, even at an entry-level job, young workers start to be tracked.

To better understand how and why Asian Americans land jobs in certain industries and how they move up in those industries, it is useful to examine the processes involved, especially the role of corporate job recruiters. More specifically, to learn how highly educated Asian Americans start their careers, it is important to determine how they found their first jobs and how they moved up to subsequent jobs.

* * *

About half of the people I interviewed were graduates of so-called Ivy League plus schools, a group that includes the Ivy League along with Stanford and MIT. Another 30 percent graduated from such selective colleges as the University of California, the University of Chicago, and New York University. For this reason, research by University of Minnesota anthropologist Karen Ho in her 2009 book *Liquidated: An Ethnography of Wall Street*, and Lauren Rivera, a professor at the Kellogg School of Management at Northwestern University, is relevant (Rivera 2015). Among the questions they examine are the following: Do graduates of elite colleges automatically get elite jobs? Does performance in college enable graduates to land the necessary initial interview? And since these Asian American students who attended the elite colleges are similar in background to those interviewed by Ho and Rivera, will they, like their interviewees, eventually get promoted so they can one day occupy the C-suites?

While many researchers focus on so-called glass or bamboo ceilings that can hobble an Asian American in midcareer, my research shows that unexpected obstacles can occur long before an Asian American worker advances to the midcareer level. As studies of women in the workplace show, when individuals start out, there are typically only small differences in jobs and salary. However, those small differences can increase incrementally and be magnified as these individuals move ahead in their careers, as Virginia Valian, a professor of psychology at Hunter College and the CUNY Graduate Center, noted in her 1999 book *Why So Slow? The Advancement of Women.* Typically, what happens at the entry level to women significantly affects what happens at the midcareer level and later.

The people I interviewed were relatively well off since they were mostly the children of college-educated parents who were gainfully employed. One would think that class would make a larger positive contribution to their efforts at being promoted, a conclusion drawn by Sam Friedman, a sociology professor at the London School of Economics, and Daniel Laurison, a sociology professor at Swarthmore, in their book *The Class Ceiling: Why It Pays to Be Privileged.*

However, race and class do not operate in isolation. For the people I interviewed, race, along with class, was still a factor when it came to entry-level jobs and at every point as they made their way up the career ladder. Even though they were mostly well off, diversity and affirmative action programs implemented by corporations did help some of the individuals move ahead.

In this chapter, I describe the intersections of individual efforts the people I interviewed devoted to finding a job, and the job recruiting and hiring programs that are offered on most campuses, along with off-site career fairs conducted by *Fortune* 500 companies and professional organizations.

Recruit and Select

When it comes to hiring for corporate jobs, there's no question that, not surprisingly, *Fortune* 500 companies are typically fixated on hiring graduates of the nation's most prestigious colleges. Even a quick scan of the calendars of Ivy League plus and selective campus recruiting offices will show receptions, panel discussions, and interview sessions with top firms for jobs in management consulting, investment banking, media, and law.[3] This is hardly surprising.

Many people would claim that graduates of such institutions possess superior abilities and high aspirations and that those qualities alone indicate why elite corporations are attracted to them. These students are already "vetted," so to speak, by the college admissions offices. Acceptance by these institutions requires a combination of superior grades and test scores, leadership roles in extracurricular activities, traits such as maturity, tenacity, and creativity, and diversity factors such as race and gender. In addition, the rate of acceptance at these schools has always been low. Although students are accepted at these institutions for many reasons, even beyond the list, including legacies, athletics, and family donations to the school, hiring graduates from these colleges would seem to guarantee that a firm will select an individual who is capable, smart, sensible, and driven. At least that is the thinking.

In the 2015 book *Pedigree: How Elite Students Get Elite Jobs*, Lauren Rivera describes how the mostly white Ivy League students she interviewed landed jobs in the highly competitive fields of investment banking, management consulting, and law. Karen Ho in her book *Liquidated* describes a more racially diverse group of students and explains how they are directed to different parts of a company—back, middle, or front—where they will have different support responsibilities, depending on where they attended college and whether they are women or students of color.

Both groups of students described in these studies were recruited by elite firms that specifically seek graduates of prestigious colleges. According to them, these graduates have a cultural fit with such firms, with employees and recruits sharing similar backgrounds, interests, and especially types of colleges attended. For example, Ho found that executives of some corporations believe that the students at certain Ivy League colleges "are the smartest and belong with their corporation who are also the smartest."

The findings by these two authors describe a framework where a firm and certain students naturally belong together. Underlying this is the assumption that at the very top, members of the cultural and the class elite fall in the same group. These students are known to have ambition and talent by virtue of attending an Ivy League school and thus represent the cultural and class elite.

Jessica, a 2000s Chinese American Harvard graduate whom I interviewed, described her job search experiences, starting with the search for a summer internship during her junior year. She told me that she felt quite confident as she walked into a reception near school hosted by a large firm that she wanted to work for. People were mingling and chatting with the interviewers, although a few of the shier students stood on the side.

"Almost immediately I recognized a few alums, and I went up to them right away," Jessica said. She knew that such events represented a networking opportunity, so she went to learn about all jobs that were available. She felt that the interviewers were bright and fun, and over the course of the semester, as she attended more of these sessions, she increasingly realized that she wanted to work at one of these firms.

In my conversation with Jessica, it was quite clear that she thought that the receptions were tailor-made for her, "an ivy graduate." The interviewers attending were alums, so there was already a shared basis for conversation about campus life, friendships, courses, and professors.

In her book, Ho also describes hierarchies that exist within both prestigious firms and the colleges from which they recruit. Along with Ivy League institutions, there are other tiers of schools from which top firms recruit, among them universities with strong business schools and technology programs and of course institutions whose students have strong personal connections with current employees of these firms, who may also be alumni.

This method of recruiting students is important in a discussion about Asian Americans because the job recruitment system that is linked with college campuses is really a sorting system for jobs. Some lead more easily to positions in the C-suites, and still others lead to better pay. Would anyone be surprised to learn that there is bias in the system?

As some of my respondents noted, they can easily get channeled to the back room where the promotion ladder doesn't necessarily lead them to the C-suites. They can get channeled into technology and internal finance and kept there. Edmund, who was mentioned in an earlier chapter, said that he found himself in a bait-and-switch situation in which he was supposed to interview for a front-office position but instead was interviewed for a backroom spot. Other participants acknowledged that they had faced similar situations, offered jobs that seemed to involve more support responsibilities than originally described.

Some of the people I interviewed told me that the jobs advertised to other tiers of colleges are not always the same ones offered to Ivy League plus students. At some of the slightly less competitive institutions, corporations may not be recruiting for what are described as the "customer-facing front office jobs." These kinds of client-facing jobs include positions in investment banking, wealth management, or sales, where an employee speaks with clients to understand their needs, and management consulting, where a worker is sent to a client for several months to do evaluations.

These jobs are valued because they usually generate the most revenue. But corporations also need to hire workers for the so-called back office, and students who get these jobs may have attended more technically oriented colleges like Rensselaer Polytechnic Institute (RPI) or Carnegie Mellon. These workers may be more mathematically and technologically inclined and may also understand critical computer and statistical analysis.

However, many functions, including research, are often revenue-generating or closely associated with the "front office." As a result, there are a range of corporate workers who could be classified as "middle office" workers. Interestingly, some of my interviewees fall in this "middle office" category. But when joining an organization, very few of them understood the different "offices" and the resulting trajectories up the hierarchy.

Thus large, "in-demand" corporations recruit on many campuses, but the many levels of corporate entry-level jobs are parceled out accordingly to the nature of different campuses. For example, Goldman Sachs may go to Harvard and Princeton to recruit for their most prestigious front-office jobs, but the company may also go to RPI, an engineering school, to recruit high-level information technology employees for middle and back offices.

As Sheila, a South Asian American 1990s graduate, told me, "I've observed that there are many more Asian Americans in the back offices, and many doing quantitative research work in all the other offices. It makes a difference because I believe that everyone who gets promoted quickly is from the front offices. The people in the back office have different opportunities."

Many sociologists, among them Sam Friedman, Daniel Laurison, Shamus Khan, and Lauren Rivera, contend that certain companies and corporations know which schools produce students who best fit certain types of jobs they need to fill and thus target graduates of these schools for recruitment.

And as indicated by many of the people I interviewed, while it may look to an outsider as if "corporations are recruiting fairly, going to many different types of colleges and giving students an equal opportunity," as one of my subjects said, and paying them almost equivalent entry-level salaries, the chances for mobility and higher salaries down the line differ significantly depending on the category into which a job falls. Thus bamboo or glass walls that deter movement between back, middle, and front offices, and bamboo or glass ceilings that deter upward mobility are constructed from the start.

Social Connections, Ethnic Connections

Many of the people I interviewed were part of extensive networks composed of Asian American friends and fellow college students who were
seeking jobs in finance, marketing, media, insurance, creative technology, and law. These networks reinforced a peer culture legitimizing
corporate work and law as valuable career options. With each succeeding
decade, as more Asian Americans worked in these areas, the playbook
contained more advice on these jobs. For the students themselves, however, it was distant acquaintances and friends of the same ethnicity who
belonged to ethnic organizations who proved the most helpful.

The immigrant parent strategy of seeking out ethnic resources and
social networks allowed job-seeking information to be shared, especially
tips on how to navigate the American career system, even if the information garnered was less extensive than that collected by other groups
whose members had more connections to individuals in the upper
echelons. The college-educated parents of the Asian Americans I interviewed, even parents who worked in corporations, knew little that was
actually helpful for their children.

While the parents may have college degrees, the majority of them
had few contacts in the professional world. Thus parents overall had
little information about even what jobs were like in corporations. While
the parents had friends, these friends rarely if ever had the contacts or
influence that could help these children get jobs, largely because these
parents and their friends did not occupy jobs in the highest levels of the
corporate world and their social networks were not as extensive as many
would assume.

My respondents benefited from all the information made available at
campus recruitment events and internship opportunities. That knowledge was passed along to members of their peer networks. Others were
members of Asian American fraternities or took part in on- and off-
campus events hosted by Asian American professional organizations,
through which they could develop skills in résumé writing, interview-

ing, and speaking and gain general knowledge of the corporate world. Many young people I interviewed also attended job and career fairs hosted by ASCEND Pan-Asian Leaders, the National Association of Asian American Professionals, the Asian Diversity Career Expo, and the Asian MBA Career Expo, along with events hosted by their own college's Asian American alumni. In other words, members of this group also relied specifically on Asian American resources to find leads, pathways, and skills that could help them find employment. As a result, even individuals who started off with few connections and knew little about how to get a foot in the door were able to rely on friends or distant relatives.

As Dave, a Taiwanese American, said of his scramble to find a job, "I panicked senior year of college. I didn't go to my college's business school, so all these finance kids were a step ahead of me with internships and everything. But I wanted to get into finance. I have friends from the business school, so I got all my information from those friends about what to put on my résumé, and I used high school connections as well.

"I even had to rely on connections from Taiwan," he continued, "like, 'Oh, Uncle Liu knows someone. Maybe he can help me out.' When it comes to finding jobs, it's all about pulling strings, especially for people from Taiwan. My friends and Asian American networks helped the most."

Despite being American-born, Dave, who was a 2000s UC Berkeley graduate, identified the importance of ethnic ties and connections that many of his relatives relied on back in Taiwan. He looked for similar social connections to help him in the United States. The ties to other Asian Americans interested in business and other corporate jobs were strong enough so that even for those students still undecided about their career track, there were others to guide them on that path. But business, media, finance, and law were not the careers emphasized in the playbook, even though it included tips on how to find jobs in those fields.[4] The playbook traditionally put an emphasis on careers such as doctor, lawyer, engineer, scientist, and so on.

My respondents typically got caught up in the frenzied search for a job that occurred during summer internships or the recruiting season for full-time jobs, feeling the pressure to find an impressive opportunity. Jobs in corporate life became natural and viable options that they pursued by participating in on-campus recruiting and attending career fairs and interviews along with their friends, especially other Asian Americans. This approach also encouraged them to further investigate the resources available to help them land a job in corporate America.

Wining and Dining: On-Campus Recruiting

Driven by the growth of Wall Street and the financial sector generally, campus recruiting, especially by financial and management consulting firms, took hold in the 1980s and became the norm by the 1990s.[5] Hundreds of firms participate in on-campus recruiting and career sessions during recruitment season, each trying to attract the best students. The carnival-like experience includes free logo-emblazoned swag—water bottles, Frisbees, T-shirts, thumb drives, sunglasses, and of course pens. Students of every age are exposed to this experience, whether or not they actually participate. Roommates or housemates discuss the sessions almost every night. Students, generally juniors, often become obsessed with these and similar recruitment events.

Students who embark on the recruitment process, like Jessica, the Chinese American Harvard graduate, introduce their friends to this path to "prestigious" and "lucrative" jobs. These corporations seem to guarantee an opportunity to work with the smartest and brightest people—in other words, people like themselves. Moreover, the relentless focus of campus career service programs on these industries and the relative simplicity of finding a job through them only serve to narrow the career options of students who lack networks of their own. Thus the second-generation Asian American is a prime candidate for this process.

There's invariably a buzz on campus about internships or highly coveted jobs that can provide summer experience and may lead to permanent employment. The majority of these jobs are with management consulting, investment banking, media, insurance, law, and creative technology firms—basically, all the service-type industries that recruit and hire talented young people who are willing to work long and often punishing hours.

Students new to the process do research and sign up for information sessions, trying to determine which firms best fit their interests. They network with one another, contacting friends who may have already worked for the firms. Those who can will contact friends of their parents who work for these firms. They question them about the interview experience, the work experience, and the organization's goals, lifestyle, and perks. Some of these students clearly have close friends or family friends in the industry; students attending the Ivy League plus colleges are pretty sophisticated. Students at the other selective colleges can also attend on-campus recruiting sessions during which representatives of firms come to campus to wine and dine prospective hires.

All the people I interviewed shared this experience, although none of them personally had any close friends or connections in the industry. The majority of my respondents were hired from these on-campus sessions, and if they weren't, they certainly attended some of the recruitment sessions that the firms offered. Except in the periods after the stock market crashes in 1987 and 2007, students had little trouble landing jobs in finance and banking.

Interviews and a Job

According to the 1980s candidates I interviewed, visiting a college career center and setting up interviews was a fairly straightforward process in their day. Nearly anyone who wanted an interview got one at the college career center.

In the 1980s Ivy League plus students and those from other selective institutions who wanted to participate in the process usually just went to their college career office and signed up with any company they were interested in. Firms included investment banks, consulting, insurance, and technology firms, and media corporations, a category that included magazines, other publishing, and television. Usually students submitted their résumés to the firms and within twenty-four to forty-eight hours, sign-up sheets with appointment times were posted. If they were lucky, and most were, they had an interview slot.

At some of the more selective schools, it was a first-come, first-served process. One person I interviewed landed all of the interviews he wanted because he "stayed close to the sign-up sheets and made sure he got the slots." Other respondents said they didn't get all of the interviews for which they submitted résumés because the process was so competitive. However, everybody got some interviews.

On average, each student met with representatives of five firms. All my respondents were then scheduled for second-round interviews, either in person or by phone. During the final round, they were often flown to an on-location, all-day interview before they were offered a job. In fact, the majority of my 1980s cohort got their jobs via a route that began with an on-site campus interview.

As Ruby, a 1980s Harvard graduate and the daughter of restaurant workers, noted, at the career office at her college there were plenty of interview spots for everyone who wanted them. She herself got seven interviews, all with firms she was interested in. Ruby estimated that representatives of at least fifty corporations visited campus during the fall semester to interview students.

Her roommates, one an Asian American, the other white, also had no trouble landing a first-round interview. In fact, most of the other 1980s graduates of select colleges that I interviewed thought that meetings arranged by an on-campus career center represented the best way to get a job; at least that was how they found their jobs.

After interviewing on campus, the lucky ones were offered an on-site daylong visit. They were flown to the company's headquarters and were scheduled to meet with one or more managers, human resources officers, and usually the highest ranking manager of the section or department they were being considered for.

As Ruby summed up the experience, "I was surprised at how cordial the meetings went, and it seemed as though they were genuinely interested in what I had to say. I was surprised, as it felt that they were trying to sell their company to me." Moreover, of the 1980s graduates who started their job searches with the on-campus process, all were offered and took their first jobs through the services offered by the campus career center. Asian Americans who attended Ivy League plus colleges said the process was very straightforward. Moreover they all felt proud because they literally believed that they got their jobs on their own.

Some respondents noted that the 1980s corporations were actively seeking more diverse candidates, including Asian Americas. There were few Asian Americans attending Ivy League plus and other selective colleges, a group that composed 5 percent to 8 percent of the student population during the 1980s, while they represented just 1.5 percent of the US population. And even fewer worked for corporations at this time.

Many from this group thought that Asian Americans, specifically themselves, were considered for affirmative action programs, just as Latinos and African Americans were. Alan, a Chinese American and 1980s NYU graduate, realized that he must have been an affirmative action hire because when he arrived at orientation for his new job, everyone there was a member of a minority group. He credits his quick rise up the ladder and later success (when he started his own investment firm) to the friends he made during this minority orientation.

Most of the 1980s graduates I interviewed thought that affirmative action was a good thing for all people of color. They mentioned the minority receptions they attended and said they felt positive about the companies that offered them jobs and in fact went out of their way to recruit them and to assign them mentors and sponsors. Some of these graduates were in managerial training programs as well. In their research, the sociologists Frank Dobbin from Harvard University and Alexandra Kalev from Tel Aviv University show that three specific types of affirmative action programs work well for women and people of color—recruitment, assigning mentors and sponsors, and management training.[6] All of these programs were mentioned by the 1980s graduates.

By the 1990s Asian Americans at selective colleges were still being interviewed by the hundreds of firms attracted by on-campus career services. And many recruiters saw broader benefits that on-campus recruiting events offered. According to one of my respondents who did recruiting at these sessions in the 1990s, "It's a great boost for the company to go to recruitment events on campus. It creates good will and gets the company name out there to new graduates. The students really enjoy the receptions, and we try to be helpful at the sessions to lure them in. When we can, we also offer a lecture on our business or on career development skills. Value added is extremely important."

During the 1990s, my respondents said, there was an increased appreciation of diversity. Diversity became the goal and embraced all racial and ethnic groups, women, LGBT groups, those differently abled, and others. One Asian American respondent acknowledged, however, that an uneasiness started to develop, even as diversity was promoted. Even though Asian Americans still represented only 3 percent of the US population, they were reaching 15 percent of the college population.

Respondents implicitly made the point to me that Asian Americans looked like the successful model minority at that time; they didn't need affirmative action, and there were plenty of them in the work world. Some respondents started to realize that they were competing against other Asian Americans for entry-level positions. Of course all of the respondents who went through this process got job offers, but they perceived some discrimination or implicit bias that they could not quite put their finger on.

By the 2000s most of the firms visiting the campuses were finance or law firms or companies eager to hire those who would go on to be part of the professional managerial elite. My interviewees recall that the number of firms visiting elite schools had increased over the previous three decades. Despite the opportunities offered by new technologies, such as video conferencing, representatives of most firms still wanted to meet students in person. Even though the number of interviewers and companies increased for on-site interviews, there was a perception that there was increased competition for interview slots.

It is possible that as more firms came to recruit, more students started to use these services. And by the 2000s it was easier to apply to many more companies. Email was available, and all it really took to apply to an additional company was just a quick edit of the application letter. Résumés were uploaded, and more students were applying to many more companies. Moreover, the hiring cycle was shorter, forcing everyone to apply and firm up jobs in the fall of the school year. By the 2000s on-campus recruiting was perceived as extremely competitive.

In the 2000s Asian Americans represented about 6 percent of the US population but made up nearly 20 percent of the student bodies of selective colleges. Yet according to my respondents, not a single one of the corporations interviewing mentioned having a particularly large Asian American workforce. In fact, most of the interviewees and especially the youngest ones observed that there were more Asian Americans on their college campus than at their workplaces. When they got to work, they were shocked to discover that they were one of only a few Asian Americans. In other words, there were proportionally more Asian American students on campus than in the professional workplace. Corporate offices seemed more prejudicial than college campuses because colleges seemed to actively seek diversity and inclusion.

On-campus interviews and the accompanying receptions at Ivy League plus colleges were clearly designed to help corporations choose future workers who shared a similar educational and cultural background as their current employees. They were also clearly meant to vet as well as attract new employees. As Rivera discovered in her study, certain qualities, especially being at ease with interviewers, represented important touchstones for candidates and interviewers. Even at this early stage some Asian American candidates were noticing that issues involving behavior could lead to bias against them. Rivera in particular cited the importance of having the ability to speak personally about one's college and life experiences because shared experiences can help connect a student with an employer.

Erica, a Chinese American who graduated in the 1990s from Yale, was one student who had no difficulties on this front because she had had an internship after her junior year in college and spent the previous semester abroad. "So, when on-campus recruiting for full-time positions in my senior year," she said, "I got interviews everywhere. I did really well and ended up getting an offer at one of the top firms. I felt really comfortable speaking about my summer work and my semester abroad. My interviewer also went to France, and we spoke about our favorite foods and about traveling throughout Europe."

Job Fairs

There are two different kinds of job fairs—on-campus and open. Both kinds entail members of firms meeting with and entertaining prospective employees en masse. Often these events are coupled with a panel discussion at which recruiters introduce their firms to students.

A student who attends a less selective college where fewer firms make on-site visits to recruit and interview may have to travel to off-campus job fairs in addition to participating in on-campus interviewing and recruiting. It's rare that Ivy League plus students go to job fairs unless they are geared very specifically to their interests. However, many students from the non-Ivy and selective schools typically attend several large job fairs. These fairs have more than one hundred top-name companies represented and thousands of students wandering about meeting recruiters and trying their hardest to be memorable. While such events can be overwhelming, people I spoke to told me that they received interviews, second interviews, and job offers via contacts made at job fairs.

A Korean American student named Phillip told me that he first heard about job fairs as a student at NYU in the 1990s. As a freshman, he attended an enormous job fair in the ballroom of a hotel in Midtown Manhattan. By his estimate there were more than a thousand people attending and more than two hundred firms represented. But he had a terrible experience—deeply intimidated by the crowds. He knew that he had to stand out, but how did one do that among thousands of people, with maybe a quarter of them Asian American and all seemingly dressed alike in a navy suit, white shirt, and red tie? In addition, he was a freshman with little experience searching for jobs. He made only a few contacts, and even they did not lead to much.

A year later Philip was persuaded by a sorority brother to attend another job fair. This time it was a local NYU event. "The sorority brother coached me and insisted that I follow his rules so as not to waste my time," Philip said. "When I walked into the room, I knew he was right. I had to stand out. He taught me how to create an 'elevator pitch'—a thirty-second summary of what I was interested in, how to make eye contact, try to keep their attention on to me, and of course dress like I wanted the job."

According to a few of the NYU graduates in my sample, the university has strong links with some of the more prestigious firms in the nation and in particular in New York City. NYU graduates did not have to attend large industry fairs across the nation and off campus. This contrasts with the arduous experience of Ally, a Chinese American who graduated from the University of Rochester in the 2000s.

Ally did not have the luxury of firms coming to campus to recruit. Instead, the University of Rochester participated in job fairs across the country. "There were no corporate receptions, because University of Rochester is not a tier 1 school," she said. "I attended these fairs in D.C., Chicago, and then New York. You submit your résumé prior to the fair, and if they like you, you get to interview with them during that fair. So not only did I get to meet a lot of companies, I got to interview.

"A lot of the job search was done on my own," she added, "by being resourceful, getting information from the career center. I remember those interviews were tough because they presented case studies that were very technical. They give you math questions you don't expect. Going into those interviews, especially in the beginning, I had no idea what I was doing, how to interview. I was pretty confused, but I figured out what to do."

Ally made it clear that her route to her first job after college was the result of independently navigating a complex path. However, most of the respondents mentioned the institutional support systems, such as campus recruitment, career fairs, and career centers, established to provide access to a variety of firms, many of which were powerful corporate players in the industry. And as Ally's experience demonstrates, depending on the competitiveness of the school, the types of opportunities available to students varied considerably.

For most of the people I interviewed, the first point of contact with elite firms was through campus recruiting or career fairs as opposed to personal connections to the industry through friends or family. Most were offered jobs after participating in the on-campus recruiting process during the fall and winter of their senior year or after completing a summer internship after their junior year.

Only two of my respondents found summer internships with the help of their parents. Two others were offered internships through minority opportunity programs, such as Sponsors for Educational Opportunity and Posse, a program that supports minorities from high school through the beginning of their career.

However, what is troublesome about young people focusing on individual effort, an approach emphasized in the playbook, is that it downplays the importance of institutional support such as minority opportunity programs and campus career support services. It also discounts the inequalities inherent in the institutionalized support systems available on campus.

Not surprisingly, students who attended select colleges had overwhelmingly positive memories of participating in robust on-campus recruitment. In addition, students from top-tier schools were more likely to find a job after a summer internship as opposed to waiting for autumn recruitment during their senior year. Thus, junior-year internships that came through formal career office guidance provided early exposure to real work experience and offered a head start when it came to forging networks in the corporate world. Individuals from lesser-known but nonetheless competitive schools found the job search much more rigorous and exhausting.

In addition, reliance on career centers and campus-aided access to companies demonstrates that despite the central role Asian American and social networks played in disseminating information about available resources and opportunities, there were limitations to this approach. For example, while in college few of the people interviewed knew established professionals who could personally refer them to specific positions or help them along in the interview process.

The job search of Ana, a young Korean women I interviewed, exemplifies how differences in college resources and mechanisms of support pushed her to find a job by reaching out to people she knew. "I found the job search hard," Ana admitted. "Coming from a smaller liberal arts school, I didn't have the same networks as people who were at schools in or near a major city. I saw myself relying on friends, friends of friends, basically my own networks, to find jobs. It was a lot of pressure on myself, me figuring it out on my own. My parents weren't able to support me, which I find is often the case for white people. But I wanted to be self-reliant, and I wanted to push for a career.

"I found my first job through a friend of a friend. I'm not sure otherwise how I would have found a job. And I also think luck plays a big role. I mean, naturally I turned to my career development center at the university. I did use that network, but it really didn't lead to much. The most effective strategy was getting in touch with people through postings of alumni and friends of friends on the school's website. I also went to career fairs at school and nearby colleges. I had to branch out. The social network that I relied on for jobs was 99.9 percent Asian, specifically Korean, and I would say those relationships were the most effective in getting leads. I had friends and professors at school who weren't Asian who tried to help me, but in terms of those who had really good and reliable leads, they were Korean, partially because we were closer."

Ana underscored the fact that her concerted efforts to connect with friends of her own ethnicity helped her find her first job out of college. She seemed to be implying that her self-reliant road to employment was the more morally correct route, compared to that followed by others who had personal connections to individuals who could make hiring decisions. At the same time, Ana downplayed the fact that she felt disadvantaged, coming as she did from a small liberal arts school that lacked the capacity or reputation to host its own corporate receptions or recruitment fairs.

She believed that extending her own capacities was the correct response to overcoming obstacles. In addition, she viewed the process of finding a job in racial terms by suggesting that her white peers often benefited from personal connections to industry insiders as well as noting that her ethnic networks were most reliable in achieving results. However, unlike the white peers she mentioned, she found that while her own connections were useful in finding reliable leads, they were not helpful when it came to finding an actual job. In other words, ethnic connections proved highly useful in locating opportunities but not necessarily in obtaining them.

Overall, upon graduating from college, the majority of my respondents were able to find a first job out of college that satisfied their personal expectations. However, when asked how they found that first job, their answers usually involved a detailed account of the incredible amount of work they devoted to the effort and elaborated on a stressful period in their lives when they felt that they had to "figure it out" for themselves—emphasizing the fact that most did not get much actual help, industry information, or contacts from their parents in the job search.

Most of my respondents mentioned but rarely seemed to value the institutional support systems, such as campus recruitment efforts, career fairs, career centers, and minority recruitment programs, designed to provide access to a variety of firms. Despite their intelligence and efforts, and despite often attending top colleges, second-generation Asian Americans typically face a range of complex challenges in finding employment after college.

4

What's in a Promotion?

A senior vice president at the investment banking firm where I worked sat me down in her office and started making some talk, asking me "How do you like the job?" Then she added, "We know that you're doing a great job, but you should make an effort to speak up more and make an effort to make people get to know you."

I discovered too late that techniques for school and college success—working hard, being smart, being the best at what you do, and not rocking the boat—were useless past junior-level positions.

—Alice, a Korean American graduate of Haverford College

How do people get promoted in elite, specialized, knowledge-based jobs in such fields as business, finance, law, and communications and media? Are there formal and informal rules at work, especially when it comes to entry-level and midlevel positions? How is the performance review, the instrument used to measure job performance, used in making such decisions?

When do workers realize that there are intangibles at work that are also taken into account, and why isn't this fact better known or shared more widely in the playbook? And clearly it isn't. Many of the people I interviewed confessed that they were shocked and dismayed to learn that intangible skills as much as measurable skills are needed to move ahead in the workplace, especially when it comes to landing higher-level positions.

According to the playbook maxims, merit is what drives promotions. But how do companies measure merit? Are intangible skills involved?

And how is the merit described in the playbook different from the merit measured in performance reviews and assessments?

The playbook tells young second-generation Asian Americans that merit involves mastering skills, working hard, putting in long hours, and not wasting time in social interactions or socializing. But in fact what matters enormously in the workplace is almost the exact opposite of what they have been told by both the playbook and their parents. Good performance at work includes all the social and leadership skills that over time help a worker form relationships to earn the trust of coworkers, both from those on higher rungs and below.

All of the people I interviewed had been evaluated with performance reviews—that is, a supervisor's evaluation of their professional performance. Performance assessments are standard in professional fields, especially in the knowledge-based industries where the people I interviewed work.

The evaluation of individual workers is continuing to evolve and will do so as long as the nature of work changes. Many of the people I interviewed assumed that they'd be evaluated as workers have always been in the manufacturing/technical economy, that is, based on whether they had the skills needed to enhance production. That approach is used early on in careers to evaluate workers in many professional fields.

But as the world continues to move to an information-based economy, workers in fields involving data, service, and finance must not only understand data but also be able to develop ways for teams of workers to perform and help these workers be more creative in combining multiple types of information.

Therefore, along with being evaluated for their technical skills, workers are increasingly evaluated as to whether they also possess leadership skills and other so-called soft skills—mostly relationship skills, such as being friendly, having empathy, listening to others, and being able to persuade people to work together. In today's economy, intangible skills are increasingly important, especially as employees move up the corporate ladder.

And as we shall see, what the playbook stresses it takes to be promoted on the job often fail to reflect what is really required. In fact, the playbook neglects the importance of these intangible skills in favor of hard skills—that is, knowledge in a particular, often technical field.

Lacking adequate parental advice, role models, mentors, sponsors, and workplace diversity programs, my respondents frequently relied on the technical skills that were once so useful in school. These job-specific skills, such as quantitative analysis, knowledge about a particular industry, writing, and presenting, evidently are not the only ones required to achieve upward mobility in a knowledge-based economy that increasingly values more intangible abilities. These include both social skills (being sociable, friendly, outgoing, and interested in people and getting team members to work together) and leadership skills (being a good listener, displaying empathy, being able to reconcile and consolidate opinions, getting other people to follow you, and being able to train managers).

Moreover, because many of my respondents lacked mentors and sponsors in the workplace, largely due to the fact that their immigrant parents were rarely professionals but were engineers and scientists with little connection to the professional world, the second generation had limited understanding of how their roles evolved as they moved up the corporate hierarchy from entry-level positions to senior management. This entailed not only possessing leadership skills but also being an integral part of a team that helps shape and lead an organization. The early performance reviews for people seeking to move up in an organization place increasing importance on hard and soft skills including leadership skills.

Older Asian Americans, those who graduated college in the 1980s and are now in their fifties, had less trouble moving up in organizations, and not simply because the nature of the workplace has changed so dramatically in recent years. Members of this generation were connected to mentors via affirmative action and diversity programs that introduced them to leaders throughout a company and to the different kinds of work required in various parts of a company.

These mentors, people who can give the employee advice, and sponsors, people who have power to advocate for the employee's advancement (for example, a person in the room when decisions about promotions are being made), also helped this cohort climb the promotion ladder by explaining what each level on the hierarchy required, especially in terms of the kinds of skills that were important to managers. At the same time, mentors and sponsors were also exposed to employees of different backgrounds with different leadership styles, making them open to people of various ethnicities and those possessing a variety of skills. Finally, sponsors actively promote their protégés.[1]

Although hard skills still matter, soft skills have become increasingly important in the modern workplace, and they involve many different sorts of strengths. After a person's first few performance reviews, typically given annually or semiannually, a manager is increasingly interested in whether the person is a team player. While managers may encourage workers to speak up in the workplace, they're actually looking for much more than that. They want workers to possess the soft skills that show that they're valuable to the team.

And these soft skills involve much more than simply being amusing and fun to hang out with while out for drinks. These skills involve getting to know what sorts of people your employee works well with, discussing shared interests, and at some point sharing details about your own family and values while learning about your coworkers' family members. It's about being comfortable being yourself and letting others feel the same way. Some refer to this sort of behavior as being "authentic."

In addition, as a person moves up the corporate ladder, leadership skills, another component of soft skills, are increasingly critical. Leadership skills involve being able to work with a team, handle conflict within a team, and listen to and inspire team members. They embrace a person's creativity in terms of devising ways to help one's company and the wisdom gained by working in a big corporation and observing its day-to-day operations.

Another important quality that helps one ascend the corporate ladder is trust, largely because trusted leaders have a greater impact within an organization. And one way to earn trust is to build relationships, take an interest in coworkers, be open, and be able to share details about one's own background and values.[2] Trust will be discussed in depth when I speak about the respondents who are in the C-suite.

While most of the people I interviewed clearly possessed the hard and soft skills needed in the corporate workplaces of twenty-first-century America, they seemed to have trouble leveraging their soft skills and leadership skills. Traditional performance reviews matter, of course. But the informal appraisals that come from everyday interactions in the workplace and the increasing emphasis on what is called 360-degree feedback, which involves soliciting feedback from a worker's subordinates, colleagues, and supervisors, are the judgments that can lead to plum, highly visible assignments.

It is in this area that many of my respondents fall short—according to their reviews. This surprised me; in my opinion, based on their interviews with me and in some cases observing them at conferences, their soft skills were amazing, and I couldn't see what they were lacking in terms of leadership abilities. Admittedly, bosses or teams who have had a long time to observe a worker might see weaknesses that were less visible to me, like an inability to trust and be trusted. Or the bosses or teams may have their own biases—for example, they may believe the "forever foreign" stereotype, as I will explain later.

Yet some of these workers complained to me about feeling excluded from meetings, being left out of important discussions over lunch, and not being invited to social gatherings with coworkers. Many of the people interviewed didn't understand why these things were happening, especially since many of them continued to believe that merit or possessing the required technical or hard skills should be the main criteria for promotion, recognition, and upward mobility in the workplace.

From Junior Level to Midlevel

When it comes to promotions in corporate jobs, the majority of the people I interviewed said that the most important ingredient was the performance review or appraisal. In annual or semiannual reviews, management uses standard criteria to measure the work that a person is performing for the company, a department, or a division. Included in these reviews are also development plans—ideas and suggestions to help the employee expand or develop abilities and skills in order to move up the career ladder.

According to older respondents, those who graduated from college in the 1980s and 1990s, most promotions up to midlevel jobs—generally vice president or senior directorships—are routine as long as people are performing the required work, increasing their appropriate responsibilities, maintaining good visibility within the corporation, and cultivating valued relationships among team members.

A person hired straight out of college is a junior-level employee for an average of five years, and each year that person earns a base salary and sometimes receives bonuses. Within the first five years some employees leave a corporation to change industries or earn an MBA. A worker in finance who returns after earning an MBA typically becomes an associate, vice president, senior director, or senior vice president—all midlevel to high-level positions.

Although the time required for a worker to move up the corporate hierarchy varies according to the organization, it typically takes from seven to fifteen years to achieve a senior executive position, such as managing director or partner with the organization. In law firms it takes an average of seven to ten years for an associate to become a partner.

In elite, specialized, and professional jobs, most employees have some idea of how far they can go in an organizational hierarchy by the time they're in their mid- to late thirties. Many people I interviewed said they thought it was important to track how their careers were progressing, and many tracked their careers by making sure they received positive feedback and revised their plans for moving forward if they were veering off course. Off track means not receiving raises or not moving forward to the next level to learn new skills.

In fact, the people I interviewed stressed that it was crucial during the first ten years to hit all the necessary marks, including performing well enough to get consistent raises, winning awards for workplace projects, being invited to workplace retreats or conferences with bosses, and being sent to leadership training, all of which are required if one wants to win a promotion.

Most of my respondents talked about how the management in their workplaces used a combination of formal and informal evaluations; that is, management considered performance appraisals but also a worker's day-to-day contributions. Performance appraisals are formal reviews that are usually completed to reward an employee with raises and bonuses in addition to a promotion. Nearly all those interviewed said that in the early years of their careers these reviews were pro forma. They allowed supervisors to list accomplishments as well as to document situations in which their work needed improvement. They were supposed to be both fair and useful.

The existence of performance appraisals suggests that a person is promoted because the company operates as a meritocracy and increases in salary and rank are given based on the quality of a person's work and the ability to advance to the next leadership role, criteria that very much echo the playbook's maxims. At least in theory, the performance appraisal is based solely on an individual's work. If you perform well or exceed expectations—meaning that you bring in enough business, support your group, complete work assignments, and maybe extend yourself on some projects—it's more than likely that you'll be promoted and receive a larger salary. This is especially true for junior employees, for whom a performance review involves a manager reviewing their productivity, the quality of their work, whether they meet deadlines, the knowledge of their work, their relationships with colleagues, including those above and below, and their ability to communicate well.

Most of the people I interviewed said that early career appraisals contain "no surprises." Employees are likely to rate themselves almost exactly as their manager. Thus, once workers have a few performance appraisal reviews under their belt, it's not hard for them to do well and get a raise, a bonus, and a promotion. In fact, my respondents said that at the junior level it was quite easy to be promoted. Also, as long as performance evaluations are positive, it's more than likely that generous bonuses will be awarded. The performance review process seemed to cause few if any problems for the people I interviewed, especially those at the junior level.

However, the early reviews lulled many of them into complacency. By doing well on the initial reviews, succeeding early on in their careers, and performing according to the appraisals they received, they believed that they were doing exactly what was necessary—for example, completing projects well and working with team members.

As a result, a large number of my interviewees were stunned when later reviews came back with criticisms, especially when they tried to move beyond the midlevel positions. A smaller group knew that their reviews weren't going to be perfect, and they'd already decided to move on to other careers. Another group thought that their reviews were fair and they were willing to work with their managers to determine ways to help them move up the career ladder.

But the group of workers who were blindsided by the reviews they received—that is, they thought that they'd get a more positive review than they did—are the most interesting to examine because their experience illuminates the gap between how workers might view their performance as compared to their employer. This group seems to think at least early on in their careers that the playbook advice is the most relevant. They are rewarded quite nicely for following the playbook advice until they want to escape that junior role. The experiences of this group are particularly revealing because they underscore the gap between the maxims offered in the playbook and the real-life requirements of the contemporary corporate workplace.

Hard Skills, Soft Skills

In any job people generally assume that how well they do depends on how well they have mastered the specific skills needed to perform the job. Those skills are typically called "hard skills," a term that embraces the specific skills and expertise required for the individual to be successful at a particular job or in a particular industry. Typically, these skills are acquired in school, at college, in specialized courses, in job-training programs, via apprenticeships, and of course on the job.

In the fields of business and finance, for example, workers need skills in basic accounting, math, and financial and spreadsheet analysis. They also need financial and market literacy. Even as executives, they need to maintain these industry-specific skills, but they must also hone social, relationship, and leadership skills.

In the field of law they need knowledge of substantive law and legal procedure, an ability to deliver clear written and oral communication and to conduct legal research, an ability to reason in an analytical and logical fashion, and organizational and problem-solving skills. To become senior partners they must retain these skills and in fact develop additional skills to help them deepen relationships with clients.

For those pursuing careers in media, communications, and marketing, jobs require skills involving data mining, data presentation, data analysis, knowledge of social media/digital communication, writing and editing, and proficiency in foreign languages. However, more companies value teamwork as workers move ahead. At the very top there is usually an executive team that leads the organization, and to get there a person needs social and leadership skills more than just cooperation to make sure that the leadership team works.

Most of the people I interviewed who went to high school, college, and graduate school and participated in work-training programs believed that they were learning what was required to do their jobs. In general, these people were required to maintain and update their general skills but primarily to be proficient in these industry-specific skills.

Industry-specific skills are highly quantifiable. They can be observed, measured, and assessed. Performance reviews for people starting out in their careers focused on such work-related elements as economic performance (the number of accounts acquired and the amount of money earned, among many other quantifiable items), contribution to the team (such as attendance and cooperation), and knowledge and ability to learn the job in question (using resources, having the necessary skills, and being able to master new skills). All of these criteria made the early performance reviews very similar to the sort of evaluations these people had encountered in school, and in fact the prescribed ways for a junior worker to move ahead in the corporate world echoed the dictums in the playbook.

However other criteria, such as communicating well with others and taking initiative, abilities also known as soft skills or leadership skills, were typically described in a narrative in their performance reviews. And as the people I interviewed moved up the corporate ladder, those narratives became more critical in their evaluations. Unbeknownst to them, as they climbed the corporate ladder and sought to become managers, partners, and directors, and to move to positions bearing other chief or executive titles, the importance of such commentary and assessments by their managers and coworkers increased.

Many of the people I interviewed disliked the consequences of such evaluations because the issues considered had little if anything to do with the sorts of things they'd learned through their entire life. Alice, the Korean American who graduated from Haverford in the 2000s and who is quoted at the beginning of this chapter, sincerely told her manager that she thought she was on the right path. She didn't need soft skills involving social interactions and leadership abilities, especially since she had been rewarded without them.[3]

Her response is typical of many of the people I interviewed. The second-generation Asian Americans had been informed by the playbook and schooled by their parents, who for quite a few, as upwardly mobile immigrants, lived and died by concrete measurements of abilities (straight As on the report card, first prize in the science fair, excellent compliments on presentations). Suddenly and abruptly they were discovering that a great deal of what they'd been taught and had believed would ease their pathway to success would not do so at all. In fact, perhaps the opposite. A whole new set of skills was needed—schmoozing, lunching with coworkers, hanging out with them after work, chatting, making small talk in the office—and by doing this they were building long-term relationships. This was a shock since these second-generation Asian Americans, like Alice, had usually started out so strong.

As one respondent said of her assessment, "My manager knows my specialized skills and knows that I am smart, but now comes the time for me to show my leadership skills in management, and all of a sudden it seems that any small thing that I did or did not do can penalize me in the assessments."

The Images: Stereotype Promise, Model Minority, Stereotype Threat

Many people are familiar with the stereotypical images of Asian Americans, which can profoundly influence opinions about this group. Some people have positive images of Asian Americans, famously regarding them as the model minority. This phrase highlights that Asian Americans achieve exceptionally well in objective measurements such as income, education, and employment.

If most people expect Asian Americans to achieve, Asian Americans can ride on this image into the work world. In other words, it will rub off positively on all Asian Americans, encouraging everyone, including Asian Americans themselves, to believe that they can be successful if they only try hard enough because rewards are linked to individual effort. However, not all Asian Americans, not even the children of immigrants, fit the model minority image. And when they fall short, they may blame themselves.

This inaccurate model minority success image is often cited to blame non–Asian American minority groups who don't perform as well as the model minority. The narrative is that African Americans, Latinos, and

Native Americans come up short in the areas of education, income, and employment because they do not put in the individual effort the way members of the Asian American model minority do.[4]

Jennifer Lee, a professor of sociology at Columbia University, has identified another relevant image, that of stereotype promise, which she defines as the promise of being viewed through the lens of a positive stereotype that leads a person to perform in a way that confirms the positive stereotype, thereby enhancing performance.[5]

This concept complements the image of the model minority. In a 2012 interview with the Russell Sage Foundation, Lee noted that because such positive images embrace Asian Americans, based on higher median household income and median education level, many people automatically confer what she described as positive bias on all Asian Americans. Thus, Asian Americans as a whole are given the benefit of the doubt and second chances because there's a promise, and an assumption, that they'll do well.

Moreover, as is made clear in a 1995 academic article in the *Journal of Personality and Social Psychology*, "Stereotype Threat and the Intellectual Test Performance of African Americans," by psychologists Claude Steele of Stanford and Josh Aronson of New York University, negative stereotypes can be internalized by anyone, including members of groups being stereotyped. The concept of "stereotype threat" is the opposite of stereotype promise. A negative stereotype, when invoked, hangs around an individual's neck like an albatross dragging that person down. Steele and Aronson's study shows that if the negative stereotype is invoked, it can even affect a group's performance on tests.

The theory of stereotype promise and stereotype threat underscores the idea that anyone can internalize a positive or negative stereotype. The positive stereotype confers advantages to Asian Americans. Thus, as the playbook says, the good will that was extended to my respondents when they were students continued through college and into the working world. Unfortunately for Asian American professionals, however, this stereotype promise didn't continue past the midcareer level.

A more relevant image comes from the stereotype content model discussed in "A Model of (Often Mixed) Stereotype Content: Competence and Warmth Respectively Follow from Perceived Status and Competition," written in 2002 by psychologists Susan Fiske of Princeton, Amy Cuddy from Harvard Business School, Peter Glick of Lawrence University, and Jun Xu from UCLA and published in the *Journal of Personality and Social Psychology*. Among other things, this model shows that groups are stereotyped not in a single dimension but in the dual categories of "competence and warmth." This theory fits the idea that people in general want to know what a person's intent is and whether that person is capable of carrying out that intent.[6]

Asian Americans in particular are stereotyped positively as to competence but more negatively as to warmth. According to the stereotype that Fiske and her colleagues found to be operating, Asian Americans are seen as smart and knowledgeable but not particularly friendly or helpful. In fact they may be seen as "too competent, too ambitious, too hardworking and simultaneously not sociable." People often place them in a quadrant where they are regarded as high in competence but low in warmth and sometimes even characterized as cold. This is also the sentiment expressed toward groups that are envied or less trusted, like Jews and the wealthy.

While members of all three groups are regarded as competent and capable, negative stereotypes are also at work. Asians are regarded as robotic, nerdy, and unable to socialize. Jews are considered cold and calculating, especially involving financial matters. The wealthy are seen as arrogant or domineering. Members of these three groups are often envied, and to bring them down a notch or make their lives a bit more difficult, they are ranked much lower on the scale of warmth and thus slightly dehumanized (see Figure 4.1).

It would follow from these three stereotypes of Asians and Asian Americans, Jews, and the wealthy that gaining social mobility (as some Asian Americans have, like my respondents) doesn't eliminate discrimi-

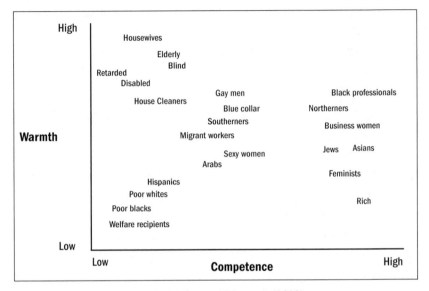

Figure 4.1. Stereotype Content Model. Source: Fiske et al. (2002).

nation based on race, religion, and class. In fact, my analysis of my Asian American respondents concludes that they're still victims of discrimination despite the fact that their families have enjoyed some upward mobility.

Results of Stereotypes of Asian Americans

All these stereotypes, both positive and negative, lurk in the background as Asian Americans try to move up the corporate ladder. Asian Americans benefit from the model minority stereotype and are also protected from some of the discrimination that African Americans face. Yet they are not regarded the same way that white Americans are. They are often overlooked when it comes to diversity programs because it is assumed that, as members of the model minority, they are successful.

However, many respondents say their parents believed that first-generation Asian Americans, who also lack proficiency in English, are the ones most affected by these models of discrimination. They say it's difficult to be "warm" when struggling to convey one's nuanced feelings. The parents' assumption is that by the time their children, the second generation, come of age, they won't be saddled with this "antisocial"/cold image.

Many second-generation Asian Americans I interviewed are particularly sensitive to the stereotype of being competent but quiet and socially awkward. It's a bias that non–Asian Americans and even Asian Americans themselves may have internalized, and it needs to be acknowledged as a stereotype. This bias resonates with Asian American adults because they have been discriminated against and rated lower on these social dimensions in the work world.

Most recently this image was an issue during the case of *Students for Fair Admissions v. Harvard*, a 2014 lawsuit that finally came to trial in 2018 and focused on whether Harvard University discriminates against Asian Americans when it comes to admission.[7] Even though in the fall of 2019 the Massachusetts District Court decided that Harvard had a fine admissions process, many involved in the suit were incensed, especially some Asian Americans and their parents who supported SFFA. They were sensitive to the image of the Asian American applicants as competent but less warm, especially when the plaintiffs charged that Asian American students were penalized in the Harvard admissions process because they got lower personal ratings despite high academic and extracurricular ratings. In its defense, Harvard showed that the number of Asian American students admitted has increased steadily during the last four decades and that personal ratings don't alter the overall portrait of who was admitted and how they were chosen. In fact, the trial findings were that the Asian American personal ratings were nearly identical to those of whites.[8]

In the corporate world, the same images are often raised in performance reviews. And like the college students, Asian American workers claim that they're victims of bias. However, unlike the Harvard case, while the number of Asian Americans in entry-level corporate jobs has been increasing, there has been no corresponding increase in the number of Asian Americans in executive jobs. Asian Americans have been characterized as lacking leadership and communication skills and warmth even though they possess extraordinarily specialized or technical skills.

The small number of Asian Americans in leadership positions sparked the popularity of Jane Hyun's 2005 book, *Breaking the Bamboo Ceiling: Career Strategies for Asians.* In response to this book, many Asian Americans I interviewed said they had enrolled in or at least read about workshops focused on landing professional-level jobs led by Asian American professionals.

Some of the organizations designed to help this population have been around for over thirty years, seeking to teach Asian Americans how to deal with these issues. Among these organizations are Leadership Education for Asian Pacifics, founded in 1982; the Asian American Journalists Association, founded in 1981; the Asian American Legal Defense and Education Fund, founded in 1974; Asian Women in Business, founded in 1995; ASCEND, a pan-Asian probusiness organization founded in 2005; and the National Association of Asian American Professionals, founded in 1982.[9]

With these resources, along with the maxims contained in the playbook, these young workers thought they were equipped to advance to the next level in corporate America. They thought that they could anticipate when they might be overlooked in the workplace and make conscious changes in their behavior well before performance reviews were handed down. They thought that they'd found ways to demonstrate their worthiness to be promoted on their own terms. However, the numbers of Asian Americans in the upper echelons of law firms and corporations are much smaller than expected, given the speed and ease with which members of this group entered these businesses as junior-level employees. Green, Holman, and Paskin write in *Bloomberg Businessweek* that fewer than a dozen Asians are CEOs in the *Fortune* 500.

How did these smart and capable young Asian Americans get themselves in this predicament? To understand what happened, it's necessary to look back at how they originally landed jobs in the corporate world. The main source of information regarding junior-level jobs came through college recruitment offices, sponsors, mentors, and of course the playbook. Other sources were members of official work groups or ethnic resource groups, along with programs designed to help Asian Americans move through the pipeline to the executive levels after they landed entry-level jobs in corporate America. These include corporate affirmative-action-type programs that seek to hire, retain, and promote people from various racial, ethnic, and other groups.

From the Front Lines

Despite the power of the stereotype as to the personality of Asian Americans, the people I interviewed thought they were protected from being tagged with this stereotype. They hardly considered themselves quiet nerds. On the contrary, when I asked them to describe themselves and their strengths, they defined themselves, for example, as "vocal, opinionated, forceful when necessary." All of them had held leadership positions since they were in high school or even earlier. Nonetheless, their managers typically tagged them as having a quiet intellect, a backhanded compliment that ironically had the effect of disparaging them. Notably, it is exactly parallel to the stereotype content model developed by Fiske and her team.

Many of the people I interviewed thought that they understood how to navigate the professional world. While they were exposed early on in their careers to the reasons why Asian Americans struggled to make their way to the C-suites and were aware of the lack of Asian Americans in high-level positions, they thought that they could overcome these problems.

The ones who graduated earliest, in the 1980s, mentioned that they had few people on whom to rely when it came to moving ahead in their careers but that over time they realized what was necessary to move up and learned that success involved more than simply doing one's best in the workplace. Many members of this group were part of training programs that targeted minority workers and groomed them to move up to leadership positions.

These were, in fact, early affirmative action and diversity programs. And independent of these programs, this cohort of Asian Americans acquired other skills. They learned to play golf, networked after work, and participated in social activities and the culture of office life. Many sought out mentors and sponsors, despite the fact that some disliked the whole idea of networking, complaining that they felt as if they were "selling themselves."

For example, a Korean American woman named SoYun who graduated from college in the 1980s said she didn't particularly enjoy going out with coworkers socially but realized that such activities built trust and encouraged empathy and sensitivity, thus making it easier for team members to have daily discussions, especially those involving difficult matters. And being able to have such conversations is a necessary skill for moving up the corporate ladder.

As I learned from the few Asian American executives I spoke to, having close relationships through shared activities allows people to get to know one another and be confident that together they can make difficult decisions for the company as a whole. In other words, social activities and shared activities allow people to build trust and confidence in one another and especially to become leaders in a company. As another high-level person I interviewed explained, "When executives look for who to promote to the C-suites, they are looking for someone to give the corporate key to." The person they share a key with will be someone they trust and have confidence in.

Parents, Sponsors, and Mentors

Of the people I interviewed, the great majority had parents who worked in the areas of science or technology, but they themselves did not. The older group of interviewees, those who had graduated in the 1980s and were now entering their fourth decade of work, along with some of the 1990s graduates, now in their third decade, realized that having parents who worked in the same industry would have helped them tremendously. For example, the parents could have warned them about such issues as performance reviews and potentially troublesome narratives that could interrupt their upward trajectory in the workplace.

Coworkers who had exposure to the corporate culture, in other words the formal and informal behavior expected in certain industries and the performance requirements in these industries, had a much easier time advancing. These coworkers often assumed that everyone around them had access to the same information. They knew what kinds of projects were preferred (for example, those that involved working cooperatively), and they had many more contacts, mentors, and sponsors even when they first entered an industry.

The people I interviewed said that the advantages their coworkers had were directly related to their parents' ability to connect them with others in the industry. These coworkers had people to turn to for advice, and these people were easily reached through personal networks. This is exactly what my respondents' own immigrant parents were lacking, and thus they entered the workplace with few contacts, a state of affairs that had a considerable impact on their own work lives and their ability to move ahead in corporate settings.

Dev, a South Asian American in his late thirties and a graduate of Harvard Law School, mentioned that his coworkers at the white-shoe law firm in Manhattan where he worked, most of whom were white, had parents or other relatives who were partners or at least associates in law firms. As a result, these coworkers learned about life in law early on. Even more important was the fact that his coworkers saw a future in being an associate or a partner because they saw other people like them in those roles. But when Dev was interviewed for his job, the firm had only one South Asian partner and only one East Asian partner.

"It's also important for performance to look ahead of you," Dev said, "and if you don't see anyone similar to you, you lose faith that it's a good long-term place or that you'll succeed here or that they'll like people like you." To him that state of affairs portended a dismal future because people have trouble envisioning a future with a company where few who look like them are promoted. As the saying goes, if you can't see it, you can't be it. Dev left the firm a year later.

Other people I interviewed located more senior classmates from Asian American alumni networks or older workers from Asian American professional organizations. For many of my respondents, however, these informal connections faded over time, and not surprisingly. Such connections are much harder to maintain because it's incumbent on the individual pursuing those contacts to stay engaged and connected. There was nothing systematic in their current framework that helped people to stay in contact with each other.

This is something many of the people I interviewed worried about. Some of them wondered aloud if they were doing enough to maintain or expand their network of mentors and sponsors. Those who were able to keep mentors and sponsors over the long haul realized the power of those connections, which could yield tremendous amounts of information, other connections, and helpful suggestions intended to guide junior people as they moved up the corporate ladder. These senior people gave advice on whether certain projects were worth pursuing, what career moves offered good exposure, and general advice about the workplace.

Connections, if maintained, also yield tremendous advantage over time, and they may also provide junior employees with what Dev said he needed so much—support and confidence. Mentors, sponsors, and connections made through parental connections often helped young people develop confidence that they could perform a particular job and that they in fact had promise. Gabrielle, a late 1980s college graduate whom I interviewed, pointed out something else: she found that when mentors, sponsors, and role models offered encouragement, she came away with the belief that their positions were something to aim for.

However, many others were stymied, despite the fact that they knew the pitfalls that lay ahead. A few years after a person joins a company, performance reviews become increasingly complex. If a person might become a vice president, a director, or a managing director, it wasn't unusual for that person to receive a 360-degree review composed of appraisals by both peers and managers.

"In a 360, it feels much more subjective," said one respondent. "It's all about your relationship to the managers and your coworkers." Another person I interviewed added, "You're evaluated by your boss and the people who worked with you and for you. Sometimes your clients can evaluate you."

It's with these more comprehensive reviews that some of my subjects start to hit ceilings. A director who moved up into a high-level managing directorship, for example, saw others fall by the wayside because of 360 reviews. He concluded, and rightly so, that the additional personal factors mattered more at a higher level. In fact, it's not unusual that relationships and how well a person manages them are implicitly rated in these reviews.

My interviewees also told me that at this point in their career it was normal to get some criticism about the quality of their work, how they worked with others, and how they handled criticism. For many of the go-getters in this group, however, it was upsetting to get criticism that seemed arbitrary and had to do with personal and interpersonal matters—and to know that these observations would be kept in their personnel files.

Reviews noting that an employee was hardworking but soft-spoken, not a team player, and lacking leadership material struck many Asian Americans as bias. For others, it was a signal to get help so they could work on their skills because they wanted to move up the career ladder. Still others received decent reviews but realized only later that they weren't assigned to high-visibility "star" projects or asked to assume leadership roles on projects that led to a large number of contacts,

sponsors, and mentors and thus a greater visibility and hence likeli-
hood of promotion.

Members of one other group, some of whom were in diversity programs, received rave reviews, mostly about their skills overall. Their
hard, soft, and leadership skills were rated positively, and their reviews
indicated nothing that could hold them back.

Sean, an East Asian who is one of the highest-ranking Asian Americans in finance, said that during his first few years as an analyst he was
branded as hardworking and smart, which seemed like a compliment.
He received bonuses and moved up to the position of a managing director. Now, however, he thinks that being considered hardworking and
smart is a great asset for anyone *except* an Asian American because it
feeds into ethnic stereotypes. This is precisely the stereotype that Susan
Fiske and her team mentioned.

In many ways Sean felt that his early years at the company where he
worked were like being in school, using math skills and learning new
ways to analyze data. "It was smarts and intellect," he said of the abilities
needed—in other words, skills like the ones "he learned in college." But
the road ahead proved rockier.

"The performance review said that I needed to speak up more. I knew
that if I were to move up, I had to change quick. That meant I had to
form better client relationships and become better in social settings. I
worked on that."

But the emphasis on improving his skills continued. "My next performance review mentioned that I had to listen more," Sean said. That
was when he realized that there were many more things his superiors
wanted him to do and that becoming a managing director involved not
only doing the work properly but also socializing, performing, being
politically astute within the workplace, and being a so-called rainmaker,
a person with a flair for bringing in new business.

In addition, the higher Sean rose, the clearer it became that his superiors wanted to promote people who defied the stereotypical Asian
American technical worker, that is, those who always followed orders

and did so without complaining. However, he added adamantly, he was already not the typical brainy type, although he was terrific in math and his early performance reviews made him sound as if he fitted the Asian American stereotype perfectly.

Sean had gone to a prominent boarding school, was an Ivy League graduate, and already had much in common with many of his higher-ups, especially on a social level. He understood that he was more like the other managing directors than like his colleagues, especially in terms of credentials if not of race. How did he make sense of this apparent dissonance?

Sean described himself as a level-headed guy, someone who got along with everyone. He believed that the firm wanted him to succeed, so he went along with their criticisms, even though he didn't think that they were deserved. For this he was rewarded. He worked hard and moved up in the corporate hierarchy. He said he had earned his success.

Was he successful because he was able to change or because he was a perfect fit, or did the organization want an Asian American? It's hard to say, but clearly Sean was able to change. And since he was someone who fit into the organization culturally, given his prep school background, he leveraged his connections to get assigned to more high-profile projects and to be given leadership roles in these projects.

Eva, a Korean American woman in her mid-thirties, reported having a similar experience, one that was even more illuminating because she was a woman. She was also an Ivy league graduate. But in the workplace she ran into problems early on.

"I practically was an apprentice or at least treated that way," she said. "And in an apprentice-type job, again, that upbringing—the behaviors that worked in college, where you work hard, head down—makes you the bosses' favorite because you work hard and you're deferential and all of those really good things. I helped whenever it was needed. I didn't mind doing admin work to get a project done. It's like you're invaluable to your boss, you make your boss look and feel good.

"Sometimes, I thought they wanted to keep me working for them because I made them shine," she added. "You're doing all the PowerPoint presentations, you're summarizing all this information, you're around to bounce off ideas. And it's almost like if you're Asian American, you're kind of built for that kind of job. But for me it was interesting because I wanted to move to the next level.

"But the feedback that I was getting was, you're too deferential, you don't speak up in meetings, you're good at analysis only," she continued. "It was really holding me from the next level even though I was also clearly friendly, had great relationships, I did speak up, my team listened to me, I could lead everyone on the team, and I was my boss's favorite." In addition, she went out socially with members of the group and was an athlete who biked with her team members.

Hers was a complicated situation. The perceptions of her and her work seemed to draw on stereotypes of both Asian Americans and women, and it was these stereotypes that made her simultaneously valuable and not promotable. She became aware of these problems and is currently working with an executive coach with the hope that moving to another company might offer an opportunity for new leadership to recognize her potential and promote her.

Dev, Sean, and Eva are just three of many young Asian Americans who hit the glass or bamboo ceiling as they sought to rise in corporate America. Sean overcame the obstacles he faced; Dev and Eva are still trying to do so. I cite them as examples because they weren't at all remarkable among the 103 people I interviewed. Broadly speaking, they were the second-generation Asian American children of college-educated immigrant parents who themselves were engineers, scientists, and doctors. Although most of my respondents, like Dev, Sean, and Eva, were not first-generation college students, they relied on the guidelines offered by their parents and the playbook. Their first reaction to the difficulties they faced in the professional workplace was disbelief. Despite the fact that they possessed all the necessary credentials, they couldn't move ahead in corporate America.

Given the broad acceptance of the playbook's maxims and how unreliable the results proved to be, I was surprised to see how many young

Asian Americans continue to rely on these maxims. And why didn't the playbook include the lessons that could be learned from these disappointments or failures?

The Playbook's Role in Promotions

While everyone I interviewed was familiar with the maxims in the playbook, not everyone followed these precepts wholeheartedly. Those who placed more faith in the playbook's maxims were more likely to feel greater disappointment when their careers didn't proceed as well as they had expected. As they would discover to their dismay, the playbook failed to spell out the so-called hidden rules that governed the workplace, rules that my respondents discovered only after they were on the job.

For starters, workers need sufficient contacts with people willing to share information about important projects, initiatives, and opportunities. In addition, some of their social contacts had to be mentors and sponsors who could speak up for them "in the room" where decisions are made. Finally, diversity programs that hire, retain, and promote people from various racial, ethnic, gender, sexual orientation, and differently abled backgrounds should be promoted among Asian Americans.

The playbook doesn't acknowledge such needs. Instead, it addresses STEM-type jobs, which are still touted as the most desirable occupations by many first-generation parents. The lack of information in the playbook combined with immigrant parents' lack of experience in corporate non-STEM jobs and the absence of role models, mentors, and sponsors make the professional promotion process seem confusing and even mysterious. The corporate jobs held by the people I interviewed are all still relatively new to second-generation Asian Americans, despite the fact that college-educated American-born Asian Americans have been holding these jobs for half a century. However, very few have made it to the top, and even when they do, there has until recently been minimal information as to why they've found it so difficult to climb these particular corporate ladders.

Most of the people I interviewed confessed that during their first year in an organization they had no idea what they were supposed to do. All the jobs these people held demanded new skills, and a major issue was how quickly a person could acquire these skills and become useful to the organization. Thus measuring the level of a person's technical skills, how hard the person worked, and how quickly the person learned was critically important when it came to early promotions. What applies to the STEM jobs and is mentioned in the playbook is that in the first few years of any position a person needs to master the actual skills required for that particular occupation.

The majority of the people I interviewed, who were graduates of liberal arts colleges, had little experience knowing what exactly was required in their jobs. They generally had a broad skill set and the ability to integrate information from many areas and to learn quickly. Companies hired them based on the belief that they were all smart and could get along with people from numerous racial, ethnic, gender, and religious backgrounds because their colleges were usually more diverse than the workplaces.

As a result, most of my respondents understood that during the first few years at a job, the emphasis is on working hard, mastering the skills needed for a particular job, being noticed, and being recognized. These junior-level jobs share many features with STEM jobs. In the beginner ranks, a person becomes increasingly proficient, something that requires days and hours of just doing the job. With experience, a person layers new skills upon earlier knowledge, giving the depth and industry familiarity required in those early years.

So it's understandable that many of the people I interviewed felt that the rules set out in the playbook had somehow been altered or hidden from them, especially since they believed that they were doing everything necessary to move up. Although most of my respondents did what their managers and supervisors wanted, the rules seemed to have changed under their feet, explaining why they failed to get the raises or promotions that they thought they deserved.

According to the maxims enshrined in the Asian American play-book, hard work, good performance, and individual effort should have the greatest influence on promotions in the workplace. The playbook suggests that accomplishments are easily quantifiable and for that reason "merit" can be both measured and rewarded. The process is compared to the one that some Asian American parents hoped would be used when their children were applying to high school or college; they simply wanted grades and scores on standardized tests to be the main criteria and those students with the best grades and test scores to be the ones admitted.

However, while the metrics used to measure proficiency at work, such as efficiency, helpfulness, quality of work, and initiative, may seem straightforward, they are not always easy to quantify. For example, on a performance review, a straightforward scale is often used to rate the quality of a person's work. When projects are of different value to the company, however, even if the quality of work put in by employees is similarly high, the optics of the metrics may be different. A perfect score on a project that isn't of crucial importance to a company may mean less than the same perfect score on a more important project.

There are also intangibles that accrue to an employee associated with a high-profile project. These include increased visibility in the company, access to important connections, and influence over important people. All of these intangibles add a great deal to an employee's portfolio and can offer a boost when it comes time for promotion.

The playbook, which reinforces the use of quantifiable metrics, makes the assumption that all Asian American professionals will do well and move to the higher levels in the workplace in a similar step-by-step fashion. However, the playbook doesn't go farther and acknowledge differences in various workplaces or the fine gradations as to why working hard may not earn a person a promotion.

By the time Asian Americans reach the midlevel in their careers, a more nuanced understanding of the work world is necessary, one that underscores the point that merit isn't just about quantifiable matters.

Merit also includes the social means a person can make use of to advance, social means that include networking, having mentors and sponsors, and maintaining the visibility of the project and team to which a person has been assigned. And yes, despite decades worth of efforts to level the playing field in corporate America and elsewhere, it can be shadowed by aspects of discrimination and outright racism.

Despite the fact that the parents of many of the people I interviewed are highly educated and worked as researchers, scientists, accountants, engineers, and entrepreneurs within their ethnic communities, they weren't able to introduce their adult children to suitable mentors. This is partly because the children were often the first members of their families to enter the corporate world. Consequently, for the second generation to learn that their time could have been better spent at a happy hour than perfecting a PowerPoint presentation represented a rude awakening.

Mike, a Chinese American who graduated from college in the 1980s, described his experience this way: "If you were used to this"—that is, the importance of social interactions—"from a very young age, it would be easy. I observed people making small talk, discussing their families, vacations, sports, but not politics." Even he, who had college-educated parents, "did not socialize this way."[10]

Another respondent, a Korean American named Dan, said that parents who were religious were more likely to have gone to church and socialized in a casual way that could facilitate these kinds of interactions, but that this pattern wasn't usual among Asian Americans. He also said that while he knew to leverage his network, others told him that they "didn't think it right to schmooze with people and then ask them for help." In their opinion, using contacts to help one get ahead may seem too instrumental. To some in this group, depending too much on a network means that a person isn't making use of individual effort. Using network ties is also not stressed in the playbook, despite the fact that in any kind of business setting most people are all too happy to tell others about how important it is to use contacts and to network.

Nicole, another Korean American who graduated from college in the 1980s, volunteered that to be noticed, especially at an event such as a cocktail party, it was important to "be deliberate" in terms of who you're speaking to and what you're saying to that person, although among most of my respondents there was a certain distaste for being so calculating while socializing. Another point to underscore is that the playbook emphasizes merit by individual effort. This does not include getting help by socializing and definitely does not include meeting and getting to know people who can offer information or who help a person get promoted in the future. To some of my interviewees, such an approach seems dishonest.

Surprisingly, they told me few playbook stories about Asian Americans who failed to get promoted and the lessons learned as to how they moved on. The people I interviewed had little knowledge about other Asian Americans who failed to move up, and until quite recently they didn't realize how common it was. Because of the lack of this knowledge and the general belief that Asian Americans are doing extremely well in the workplace, given that they have the nation's highest median income and education, those who struggled thought that they were the exception, the "only one" who didn't get promoted. Why else would the playbook not include more information about this issue? Why else would no one discuss it?

Some of my respondents also assumed that for Asian Americans social and upward mobility erases racism. Since as a few said they were able to live in mostly white middle-class neighborhoods and attend mostly white schools, they didn't really have the same kinds of problems as blacks or Latinos. Thus, the logical conclusion for them was that they were read as more similar to whites and thus less of a minority and less of an afflicted class. Thus some didn't realize that racism was so stubborn and that it would indeed affect Asian Americans, at least in corporate America. Because of this belief, they had no language to express racism against Asian Americans. And for that reason the issue isn't mentioned so much in the playbook. As a result of which Asian Americans, when confronted with racism, especially in the workplace, simply assumed they were guilty of personal failures, or that any racist incident was just an interpersonal conflict and not something more widespread and systemic.

In addition, the people I interviewed had little understanding and few workplace plans about how to overcome setbacks, a critical issue when it comes to making one's way up the ladder in corporate America. Neither their parents nor the playbook had much to say about how to proceed when they hit ceilings in the workplace or were frustrated by a failure to obtain promotions or raises. Since the playbook offered little acknowledgment of the fact that people fail but then move on, or even that they might and often do fail in the workplace, some of the people I interviewed rarely shared their disappointments when they struck roadblocks in their careers.

I believe that this pattern is part of what I call the "shame game," something many Asian Americans must confront and deal with. When a person "fails"—and the idea of failure incorporates many things, even a missed opportunity—that person is often unwilling to discuss how to solve the problem or move on in a realistic and productive way. One respondent bluntly said of not being promoted, "It's really just about what I did or didn't do"—in other words, totally his fault, even if other more powerful factors—like racism or discrimination beyond his control were at work. In fact, many of the respondents admitted feeling this way, especially women who thought that their own poor performance was the cause of not getting promoted.

That is because they feel ashamed. They would rather "save face" by repressing their failure, not discussing it or even mentioning it to anyone, including and perhaps especially their parents, except to say that they were doing just fine. This approach is reflected in the playbook. Among Asian Americans there is a silence about personal failures in the corporate world, a state of affairs that only compounds a sense of helplessness because the playbook emphasizes self-reliance.

However, despite the playbook's emphasis on individual effort, the majority of the people I interviewed still turned to friends, mentors, sponsors, or executive coaches or sought advice from Asian American employee resource organizations and professional development groups. Making use of these connections wasn't considered a violation of the time-honored tradition of self-reliance. Rather, approaching these groups and individuals was seen as making individually initiated requests for help involving self-improvement. Making these requests was considered being self-reliant, and if that wasn't exactly the case, the fact was neatly overlooked.

On the other hand, some of the people I interviewed had access to a more systematic way to get explanations and help when it came to addressing the inevitable bumps in the workplace. Specifically, they had deep connections to minority professional groups and diversity and affirmative action programs. This allowed them access to a system or organization that allowed them to seek advice from people with whom they were familiar. They had better connections than the group as a whole, and as a result they got helpful advice more quickly.

At the same time, the younger graduates were reluctant to reveal that they used these kinds of affirmative action programs because they feared being stigmatized. The narrative they believed was that affirmative action programs gave people a leg up and that often that leg up was undeserved, a narrative also sometimes believed by people who were not helped by affirmative action programs and thus often resented them as providing an unfair advantage. Thus, even people who had the benefit of affirmative action and made use of diversity programs felt very self-conscious about it and discussed their participation in such programs only with people who seemed sympathetic to the idea.

Jim, a Chinese American who graduated from college in the 2000s and was also a fellow of the group Sponsors for Educational Opportunity, which provides mentoring, told me that while he might have benefited from affirmative action or diversity initiatives, he avoided any possible negative impressions that he might have had an unfair advantage by simply avoiding the topic. His comment reflects a wider sentiment that individuals might not be qualified if they made use of "that kind of help."

The experiences of these second-generation adult workers in the corporate world complicate the upward path that we assume most Asian Americans would take. Clearly, there was no single path to success, and any path could be rocky and circuitous. The most important message is that the real story and framework wasn't told in the playbook nor even shared among Asian Americans themselves. And for many Asian Americans, that was a tragedy.

5

Moving Up to the Corner Office or Close to It

I'm just not a fan of socializing, but I know that it's important to
get to know my colleagues. When coworkers talk about problems
at home, it's much easier to talk about problems at work too.

—Heide, Korean America 1980s graduate

THE challenges Asian Americans face in their efforts to move up the
ranks in the corporate workplace are, as we have seen, considerable.
Despite the odds, however, a few Asian Americans have managed to
achieve this goal, and their experience offers lessons that are immensely
useful for those on their way up.

Along with these seven individuals, I included in my discussion three
others who were fast approaching those positions, as well as some of the
coaches, mentors, and sponsors of this high-level group, who offered a
somewhat different perspective from the corporate workers I focused
on.

Of the workers I interviewed, nearly 7 percent occupied executive
offices. This is almost exactly the percentage of Asian Americans in
corporate leadership positions nationally. According to the 2017 Colby
article in *Bloomberg*, Asian Americans constitute 12 percent of all professionals, regardless of their race, but only 5 percent of Asian American
professionals are executives.[1] Among American CEOs, even fewer Asian
Americans can be found. In 2017 fewer than a dozen of the CEOs in the
Fortune 500 companies were Asian American.[2]

These figures seem glaringly low when compared to the percentage of
Asian Americans in higher education, especially Ivy League institutions.
While Asian Americans constitute close to 7 percent of the US popula-
tion, they represent over 20 percent of the undergraduate population at

America's elite colleges. More than a quarter of Harvard's class of 2023 are Asian American.[3]

These statistics raise a provocative question that was asked at the beginning of the book: Why are there so few Asian American executives when so many of them have graduated from elite colleges and by all rights should have made their way up the corporate ladder?

Of the more than one hundred young Asian Americans I interviewed for my research, only seven had reached the C-suites, occupied by such company leaders as the chief executive officer, chief information officer, and chief financial officer, or such equivalent executives as executive vice president and general manager. Regardless of the exact title, these men and women were part of the executive leadership team heading the organizations for which they worked.

These seven all had undergraduate degrees from Ivy League colleges or other elite and selective institutions, among them MIT, the University of California, Berkeley, and the University of Chicago, along with MBA or JD degrees earned in the 1980s and early 1990s. All are in their late forties or fifties, and all but one have parents who attended college. At least two have parents or extended family members who were high-level executives in large foreign or global corporations.

The group included two Korean Americans, three Chinese Americans, one South Asian American, and one Japanese American. Two of the seven are women. This is a very diverse but elite group, and the timing of their parents' arrival in the United States reflects the early immigration patterns of the 1960s and 1970s, when immigration laws were made less restrictive and rewritten to allow large numbers of Asians to immigrate. Specifically the Hart-Celler Act of 1965 (also known as the Immigration and Nationality Act of 1965) was passed. The fact that all but one of the respondents was a first-generation college student (the first in the family to go to college) is significant and raises a question: If parents enjoy a high socioeconomic status and have college degrees, what qualities are transferred to a child? It seems that important advantages are transferred to their children since most of the respondents of this elite group are not first-generation college students. In addition, two of the seven people in this group had fathers who were high-level corporate executives with roots in their homeland, which raises another important question: What benefits are accrued by being a child of an executive?[4]

As Shamus Khan and Lauren Rivera have argued, the elite will reproduce the elite.[5] A child of a corporate executive will fare better in the corporate workplace than the child of a lower-level worker. The two children of Asian executives in my respondent group became executives themselves. They were exposed to more corporate role models among their parents' friends, and partly as a consequence acquired more of a sense of how one operates and makes one's way in that world. In other words, they followed their parents' footsteps.

When I first asked my seven high-level interviewees how they got their jobs, they all replied by telling me that they were just really good at what they did, especially when it came to getting results from the people who worked for them. That response wasn't surprising. Members of this group would be expected to be major contributors to and capable leaders of the corporation.

One respondent, a Chinese American named Ben who was a partner in a white-shoe law firm, emphasized that he was just like the other members of his leadership team except for his race: they were all white, but he was Asian American. "Look at me and what I do," said Ben, who graduated from college in the 1990s. "I'm not so different than my colleagues except for the color of my skin."

Like many of his Asian American peers in the corporate workplace, Ben possessed the credential of an Ivy League education, as did his wife, who was also a lawyer and worked for a large firm. The couple's three children attend private school, the family lives in a luxurious apartment on Manhattan's Upper East Side, they attend church regularly, they donate to many social causes, and they support the arts.

Others in this group also emphasized the fact that they had much in common with the other members of their leadership teams. Grace, another Chinese American who graduated from an Ivy League institution in the 1990s, said that she doesn't believe in bamboo ceilings because she thinks that they give people an excuse not to try. She does, however, believe in strategic networking. She "purposely, strategically emphasizes and highlights" what she has in common with the others, she said, adding, "We're all different, and we're all bigger than our pedigree."

All of these Asian American leaders had much in common. As mentioned, all graduated from Ivy League or similar institutions. Their children go to the same schools, very often private schools. The parents see one another on athletic fields and at the pool, the gym, the field, or the lake when their children compete against one another in sports. They are all members of the same boards of cultural institutions. They even go to church together.

At first glance it would seem as if the Asian Americans in this elite group were just like their non–Asian American counterparts, a population that the sociologists Richard Zweigenhaft of Guilford College and William Domhoff of UC Santa Cruz described in their 2011 book *The New CEOs: Women, African American, Latino, and Asian American Leaders of Fortune 500 Companies.* The main difference between the high-level Asian American executives I interviewed and the other CEOs discussed in the book involves racial or ethnic background.

We know that the number of Asian Americans decreases as workers move up the professional ladder. However, it's hard to explain exactly why this is true. Is it implicit bias at work, or racism, or discrimination? Or are there some aspects of the corporate workplace that prevent Asian Americans from ascending? The explanation is elusive, but to seek an answer it is important to explore the critical issue of trust, how to build it, and what the issue reveals about how people make their way up the corporate pipeline.

The Importance of Trust

Given the elite background of my second-generation Asian American respondents who are executives—two are children of executives, all but one of their parents have college degrees, and they all attended Ivy League or other selective colleges—it would have been easy to conclude that when it came to their success in the corporate workplace, it was simply a matter of class reproduction—the elite reproducing the elite.

However, that conclusion would not be wholly accurate, given my conversations with this particular group of Asian Americans. When I asked them to explain how a leadership team works, they told me that for executives occupying corner offices, it was especially important to communicate both with one another and with other members of the corporation. How well they communicated, how often they communicated, and how they worked together as a team mattered considerably.

As I discussed in earlier chapters, there exists a set of skills that the playbook never covered. These skills include the abilities to be seen as warm, to possess social abilities, to be able to converse well with others, and to have other capabilities beyond simply being competent and hard-working. To be promoted, to be respected, to be credible, and to lead, it is clearly important to demonstrate warmth as well as expertise.

However to become an executive, warmth also involves being seen as a member of the so-called in-group and thus someone to be trusted. This is why journals on management and organizations frequently examine the issue of trust. For example, in the 1998 article "Not So Different After All: A Cross-Discipline View of Trust," written by Denise M. Rousseau, Sim B. Sitkin, Ronald S. Burt, and Colin F. Cameron, the authors devoted an entire issue of the *Academy of Management Review* to examining the academic fields that consider the issue of trust. Among other conclusions, they found that trust is needed, both within and between organizations, that it is multilevel (extending among individuals, groups, companies, and institutions), and that it is affected by organizational change. The authors define trust as "the willingness to be vulnerable under conditions of risk and interdependence," adding that trust varies as the relationship between individuals alternates between seeking security and achieving self-sufficiency.

John K. Butler Jr., in his 1991 article "Toward Understanding and Measuring Conditions of Trust: Evolution of a Conditions of Trust Inventory" in *Journal of Management*, concluded that trust is important in building a healthy professional relationship with one's colleagues, a relationship that in turn can help a person move up the career ladder. Trust is also an important ingredient when it comes to management and leadership. It is generally agreed that for men and women to have satisfactory relationships with one another, trust is essential.

And it's not just academics writing about trust. The 2019 book *Trillion Dollar Coach: The Leadership Playbook of Silicon Valley's Bill Campbell*, written by three business executives—CEO Eric Schmidt, senior vice president Jonathan Rosenberg, and director Alan Eagle—also addresses the issue of trust at the highest level of a business organization and how and why it is essential to the organization.

Trust develops over time. When someone trusts another person, whether in business or in one's personal life, the first person becomes more vulnerable. That person reveals more to the other person because the first person has confidence in the other person's dependability, judgment, and more. It makes perfect sense that the high-level executives I interviewed underscored the importance of trust at this level.

These ideas were expanded by Susan Fiske, professor of psychology at Princeton University, in an article titled "Stereotype Content: Warmth and Competence Endure," published in 2018 in *Current Directions in Psychological Science*. In that article she linked warmth to friendliness and trustworthiness and competence to capability and assertiveness. Her research showed that Asian Americans who are rated low in warmth are also rated low in trustworthiness (see Table 5.1, taken from Figure 1 on page 68 of the Fiske article).

Thus since there is a relationship between warmth and competence, there is also a relationship between trust and competence. Perceived

Table 5.1. Susan Fiske's 2018 Stereotype Content Model: Warmth and Competence Endure

	Low Competence (Capability, Assertiveness)	High Competence (Capability, Assertiveness)
High Warmth (Friendliness, Trustworthiness)	**Common**: Elderly, Disabled, Children **United States**: Italian, Irish **Emotions Evoked**: Pity, Sympathy	**Common**: Citizens, Middle Class, Defaults **United States**: Americans, Canadians, Christians **Emotions Evoked**: Pride, Admiration
Low Warmth (Friendliness, Trustworthiness)	**Common**: Poor, Homeless, Immigrants **United States**: Latinos, Africans, Muslims **Emotions Evoked**: Disgust, Contempt	**Common**: Rich, Professional, Technical Experts **United States**: Asians, Jews, British, Germans **Emotions Evoked**: Envy, Jealousy

The four quadrants in which people fall. For example, Asians (along with Jews and the rich) are in the quadrant with low warmth and high competence. Groups in this quadrant evoke the emotions of envy and jealousy.

trustworthiness is clearly an important ingredient when it comes to a person's general evaluation of another person, although only if that person already possesses the necessary competence.[6]

Fiske further emphasized how her stereotype content model can be used to explain some of the stereotypes associated with those who fall in so-called ambivalent categories, people like Asian Americans, who are viewed as smart but cold and therefore less trustworthy. As we have seen, the stereotype content model has two dimensions, one measuring competence and the other measuring warmth. Asian Americans were rated as being highly competent but lacking in warmth.

This finding was repeated in many of Fiske's studies. She and her colleagues found that people both admire and resent competent but cold individuals. Resentment sometimes caused envy, and there were additional risks associated with being envious, one being that a person envied is less trusted since that person may be viewed as a foe rather than a friend.

These sentiments were expressed by Sam, a South Asian who graduated from an elite college in the 1980s and holds a master's degree in business administration. As Sam, who grew up in the suburbs and whose parents have college degrees, said of the role of trust,

> When I hire someone for the executive team, I'm looking for someone who I can trust. We need to know that he or she has our back, and we have theirs. We can have disagreements one day while still needing to vouch for each other the next,

and we want to be able to have a sense of what this person will say or do in most situations—to know his values. We want to be comfortable in working with each other. When executives look for who to promote to the C-suites, they're looking for someone to give the corporate key to. And what that means is that this person will be able to close the door, open the door, and keep the organization safe. They need to know how to use that key.

When executives promote someone to this level, it is akin to giving them a key to the organization. The person needs to know how to use that key to keep the organization safe—like being a gatekeeper when necessary. The person executives share that key with must be someone they trust and have confidence in. Of course, at this level there are plenty of competent people to choose from—remember all the young men and women with hard skills—but many fewer whom executives feel that they can trust.

By the time an Asian American reaches the executive level at an institution, the dictums of the playbook have been mostly abandoned, especially since it did not offer advice about soft skills, social skills, or tangible "tools" beyond simply "working hard," according to a Korean American mentor/sponsor/coach named Nicole who graduated from college in the 1980s. So few Asian Americans can be found at a high level that information about them and advice from them is hard to come by.

As we've seen, it's important for a person seeking to be promoted to be seen as warm and to possess social, leadership, and other abilities beyond being smart and capable in one's specific area of work. To move up, to be respected, to be credible, and to lead, a person must be able to demonstrate both expertise and warmth. However, to ascend to the executive level, warmth is, by extension, seen as an indicator that a person is trustworthy and a member of the in-group.

Being Trustworthy

To be trustworthy and to build relationships, a person must have contact with the people that he or she is trying to relate to. It is also important to share and to let other people know that you care about the things they care about. It is important to be warm.

As the people I interviewed recalled their early days in the corporate workplace, some confessed that they had trouble socializing with their colleagues and in particular discussing personal matters at work. For many, the playbook emphasized not showing one's personal side at work. One person who expressed these feelings was SoYun, a Korean American who graduated from an elite university in the late 1980s. Early on in her career she overheard colleagues discussing their children in the office. At the time she thought that subject was too personal to be discussed in the workplace. But today, as an executive, she has clearly changed her mind.

"It's pretty much a requirement to be comfortable to speak about all kinds of matters," SoYun said, "especially your children." In fact, she now understands why sports, travel, and even the weather are such great conversation starters. Once you start speaking about these topics, she has come to realize, it's much easier to continue a conversation until two people find common ground and eventually build a relationship.

Trust among members of a leadership team is extremely important. As Sam, the South Asian who graduated from college in the 1980s, made clear, it's necessary for the members of the leadership team to trust one another. In fact, all of the highest-level workers whom I interviewed said that trust was vital. They acknowledged that achieving trust among the entire leadership team was sometimes difficult, but they felt that they themselves were trusted by their companies' inner circle.

SoYun elaborated on the subject of trust and how it was achieved over the years: "You have to develop that trust over time," she said. "They are not going to trust you on day 1; you develop the trust. You go to more meetings, and you get more face time. They have to trust that you are competent. They have to trust that you will be giving them good advice. You've got to have the desire to do what's right for the company. This is the body formulating policy and approving strategy. The board needs all the facts and all the pros and cons to figure out the risks. They need good counsel. Anyone they let into the boardroom they have to trust."

On the executive level, trust among people begins on a personal level. People have to know a person well in order to promote the person, especially when it comes to promoting someone into the inner circle of the leadership team. As the people I interviewed pointed out, finding commonality and making connections were crucial. A few of the people I interviewed added that to trust is to be honest and open, to be able to feel comfortable enough to disagree, to argue, and to respectfully come up with a common plan behind closed doors.

Another person said that to be able to trust meant that an individual had to understand where others were coming from and have the ability to relate to them. One way to do this was to show that you and the other person were alike in many respects.

Being Authentic

A few of the people I interviewed raised the issue of authenticity. Although they wanted to fit into the corporate workplace, they also wanted to be authentic. They wanted to emphasize the way that their race made them different from other people, even people of other races and ethnicities who have experienced discrimination.

Jack, a Japanese American finance executive from the Midwest who graduated from college in the late 1980s, said he believed that people had to be true to themselves. So as a visible Asian American, he explained, he needed to demonstrate his Asian Americanness. For example, when he started work at a large firm in the late 1980s, a time when many of his coworkers knew little about Japanese food, he frequently took them to interesting Japanese restaurants.

At his current job, when he and his colleagues traveled to Asia, he "showed them the best places around, even though most restaurants were new" to him too, especially since he was American-born. But he felt that he could be at least a partial "cultural translator." This was a truthful representation of himself, Jack thought, and he believed that this openness and vulnerability allowed his colleagues to see him as he really was.

Jack knew that his team members accepted his version of his Japanese American self. He made it clear that while he was thoroughly American, like the other team members, he could explore other cultures. He also made it clear that he would support others in the company if he saw discrimination. As a result of such actions, his fellow executives trusted him, he said, and he in turn trusted them.

For Asian Americans, authenticity is a critically important issue just as it is for other racial groups. However to be trustworthy one has also to been seen as warm. One way to be seen as warm was to be personal, be caring, have empathy, and be authentically Asian American—however one chooses to be.

The executive team typically knows that Asian Americans bring to the workplace qualities that are good for the team—for example, good education, critical thinking skills, even STEM skills, and good work ethic. They want Asian Americans to be seen in a positive light so as to attract business from the Asian American community. But to be authentic is to not hide one's background. On the contrary, a person should make use of that background and help others understand it, it is increasingly believed. Especially in an ever more diverse business world, people with different backgrounds can bring different ways of seeing the world, which in turn benefit the business.[7]

As Jack noted, he sees his background as an asset that can be used to achieve positive results. Jack believes that he brings a great deal to his employer. He has presence, confidence, and poise. He is unusual in that he is one of only two of the people I interviewed whose father was, like him, an executive of a multinational corporation.

Being authentic also means that Asian Americans don't have to waste time and energy figuring out a way to present themselves at work that they think will be acceptable. As Jack said, he "didn't need to hide behind that model minority." Authenticity means you can go to work and be yourself. If your own race and authenticity is hidden and only sameness is stressed to the executives, then why promote an Asian American or let an Asian American ascend to a C-suite? In other words, what does being an Asian American bring to the company?

As America becomes increasingly diverse, despite a growing presence of people opposing diversity and supporting homogeneity, reflecting the stance of President Donald Trump, and his virulent opposition to multiculturalism, it's progressively desirable to express one's authenticity around, food, dress, and activities. An increasing number of groups have been doing this, and it has pushed workplace relations forward. It's difficult to work while hiding something about yourself. This impedes trust and the relationships one has with others at the workplace.

How Does a Person Build a Trust Fund?

Amy Cuddy, a professor of social psychology at the Harvard Business School until 2017 who now teaches at the Harvard Executive Education Program at the Business School, was a student of Susan Fiske's and still works closely with the stereotype content model. According to Cuddy's research, discussed in her 2013 *Harvard Business Review* article, "Connect, Then Lead," written with Matthew Kohut and John Neffinger, and in her 2015 book *Presence: Bringing Your Boldest Self to Your Biggest Challenges*, when a person first meets another person to establish a business relationship, trustworthiness matters even more than skills and competence.

From an evolutionary perspective, Cuddy wrote in her book, "it is more crucial to our survival to know whether a person deserves our trust," adding, "Before people can display their business skills, they may have to demonstrate that they can build great relationships, that they can influence others in a positive way, and that they can make people feel better. Once these relationships have been established, people can demonstrate their strengths" (2015, 72). If someone you're trying to work with doesn't trust you, you can't get far. But if you become trusted, your skills and intelligence become less of a threat and sometimes even an asset to the relationship.

Cuddy's research underscores the importance of trust in executive offices. Yet while all of the executives I interviewed agreed that trust is extremely important in the corporate workplace, aspiring Asian Americans are only now discovering how significant a role trust plays in such settings. This is especially true at the midcareer level. Employees at this level initially didn't think that trust mattered at all when it came to getting a foot in the door. However, looking back over these executives' stories, it is clear that they were seeking in their own ways to build trust throughout their careers, even if they weren't consciously aware of its importance.

Asian American Executives and Developing Trust

A trust fund is a savings account of good will that is your reserve to withdraw from when necessary. My respondents told me that friendships among coworkers, and especially friendships with executives, create good will. Many of the people in these relationships do not spend a great deal of time together outside of work, but they do socialize. Their families may see each other a few times a year. Their children may see each other much more often. These relationships allow upwardly mobile executives to see their executive team members in other settings. These aspiring executives are not at all opposed to mixing work with socializing, which they believe is important when it comes to getting ahead. And of course they spend plenty of time together at work.

The ways that the people I interviewed got to know the executives they worked for are idiosyncratic and personally distinctive. For example, a Korean American financier named John who graduated from college in the 1990s believes that playing sports throughout his youth was critical to his success in the workplace. "You learn how to function with others being a part of a team sport or individual sports," he said. "To me it's an important part of someone's makeup. It shows a bit of competitiveness and kind of shows how you react to situations. . . . It's a point of connection," he added, especially to colleagues who also played sports.

John was quickly recognized for all the effort he put into his assignments, including working long hours and bringing in deals. In fact, he was tapped for a leadership rotation early on. At the time the executives in his corporation had instituted a strategy to increase the number of minorities at the company's highest levels. They developed a pipeline program under which the executives would choose minority employees showing high potential to rotate through various divisions of the corporation so they could work with the company's leadership.

John was one of the early recruits. Only later did he learn that these programs were a way for senior leadership to evaluate which members of minority groups could be fast-tracked to higher positions while also exposing them to a variety of leadership styles throughout the company. Initially John was not a fan of the idea, but when he realized the important information and feedback that he was getting, he became a great supporter of the effort. This program, in effect an affirmative action program, allowed him to make connections with various executives across the company, thus easing his way up the corporate ladder.

Many other techniques were available to help workers get to know their coworkers. Almost all of the people I interviewed urged others to find out what activities their boss or team members liked to do. As Ben, the Chinese American, suggested, "If they liked to go drinking, go drinking. If they love playing golf, learn how to play or go play golf with them. If they like vacationing, perhaps plan a trip to the same place, and go have a conversation with your boss and ask him what his travel suggestions are." The goal, he added, was not to be obsequious but to find something you had in common with your colleagues in order to bond with them. As Ben had realized early on, except for the factor of race, he was exactly like the other executives at his company.

Andy just believed in networking. After becoming a vice president, he figured out that it was important for Asian Americans simply to network. In fact, he said that Asian Americans he met were "so bad at networking" that he "just wanted to set up ways that they could learn how to network." As he put it, "They could network about anything. There was no need for a cause. They need practice."

Tim, a 1990s Ivy League graduate, mentioned another technique. Tim said he learned how to network starting in his junior year of high school when he was a fellow of Sponsors for Educational Opportunity (SEO), a program designed to help minority students make their way through high school and college. The program introduced him to a mentor who worked with him throughout college and beyond. After college, using the skills he had learned from his mentor, Tim found other "rabbis" who eventually became his sponsors.

This approach was not something he learned at home. Although Tim's parents were college educated, they never taught him any networking skills, nor were they comfortable in situations where they had to make small talk. His parents disliked the whole idea of networking, in fact; the exchange struck them as too transactional and even distasteful. Perhaps networking seemed to belie the playbook notion of individual effort. Because his parents were not helpful in this regard, Tim modeled himself after the people he met through SEO and his so-called rabbis. These people were confident and self-assured. They "owned the room when they walked in," as he put it. He aspired to be like them.

Asian American women, of course, socialized somewhat differently than the men. A Chinese American named Grace, who graduated from college in the 1990s, noted that on her way up the corporate ladder she found an easier way to socialize, and to do so on her own terms. She did not like going out at night drinking, she said, because she had children. "So I came early to work," she said, "and read newspapers on a coffee table outside of my boss's office." She politely asked him if he minded her doing that, but explained that since she was a news and sports junkie, she wanted to read all the papers first thing every morning, and there they all were in front of his office.

Sometimes she brought in homemade baked goods, which everyone appreciated, and through conversations about sports and the news, she got to know the executives and other members of the firm quite well. In her own way she was behaving in an authentic fashion, and she got closer to the executives in her firm in a way very different from the one previously imagined for women. Grace was also a beneficiary of the work of the Posse Foundation, an organization that provides college tuition support along with faculty and career mentoring. After acquiring various leadership skills through Posse, Grace learned how to be a mentor herself.

The strategies used by this small group of executives demonstrate that they clearly excelled at doing what was necessary to keep moving up the executive ladder. Nicole, the executive turned mentor/sponsor/informal coach, offered this advice to young people who wanted to become executives:

> You need a lot of people [mentors, sponsors, and supporters] in your corner and that takes a lot of cultivating. And it can take very deliberate cultivating. I think there are some people who are just naturally really good at it. They can talk to anyone. They kind of instinctively know who's up and who's down, who's good, who's bad, who's going to help and who's not going to help.
>
> And I think that there are many people who aren't instinctive—and it's hard work, especially if you're not a natural at it. So because it's so hard, it falls to the bottom of our list of things to do because we don't think it's fun. You kind of have to get over it and accept it and practice. Asian Americans are very good at practicing things.

These particular C-suite leaders are exceptional in their ability to build trust and to create and maintain social relationships. As they made their way up the career ladder, they learned how to deal with coworkers, both those above them and those below. However, in discussing their career trajectory, very few of them highlighted their ability to socialize and maintain relationships as one of the qualities that got them hired in the first place.

In fact, all of these executives and most of the people I interviewed emphasized that the early years of their careers were packed with projects that showed off their skills, intelligence, and competence. During this period they emphasized their ability to work hard.

As we have seen, soft skills didn't become truly important until the midcareer level. Now, as executives, they realized that they possessed a web of influential social relationships that made use of their soft skills. In analyzing their work trajectories, these Asian American executives acknowledged that they had indeed created relationships and established trust with others, starting on their very first day on the job and sometimes even before. Perhaps having soft skills was just as or even more important during those first few years.

Amy Cuddy and her colleagues Matthew Kohut and John Neffinger in their 2013 *Harvard Business Review* article "Connect, Then Lead" clearly argue that warmth facilitates communication and trust and that to lead, one needs to combine warmth and competence.

The Lack of Trust

Clearly, developing the trust of one's colleagues leads to considerable benefits. And the reverse is also true: the lack of trust can lead to serious problems in the workplace. When executives don't trust one another, they generally spend a great deal of time and energy protecting themselves rather than protecting the company for which they work. If this is happening among a small group at the top, it disrupts work. If there is little trust among the executive team, each member of the team will do as he or she pleases. If there is trust, however, a genuine conversation, even one that includes disagreements and differences, can occur over time and some sort of consensus can be reached, even when there are hard decisions to be made.

Dan, a Chinese American banker who graduated from college in the early 1990s and is actively trying to leave his current job, told the following story. He and the other members of the leadership group were getting ready for a quarterly divisional meeting the following week. He had been to many such meetings before. They were generally routine, and his team was usually briefed on the most important announcements. However, at this meeting, it turned out that he was the only member of his leadership team who had not gotten briefed.

Dan was stunned and shaken by the incident. And he could not figure out why this had happened, unless it was a deliberate slight. To him this felt worse than not being invited to play golf with his colleagues since that was "just a social invitation." He was doing work that he loved, and he felt betrayed by the people he trusted. He couldn't understand why he had been left out, especially since he was at the pinnacle of his career.

Situations like this, and worse, play out at all different levels of corporations, I was told by the people I interviewed. What happened to Dan might have simply involved a personal run of bad luck, but it might have been connected to a general view of Asian Americans that is ingrained into the corporate culture, the stereotype content model's "cold and competent" stereotype of members of this group.

A corporate culture can define how employees relate to others and especially to minorities such as Asian Americans. Corporate culture embraces the values, beliefs, and behaviors that help determine and guide how the organization functions on a day-to-day level as well as how the corporation approaches customers and employees. This corporate culture is laid on top of the shared trust among the leadership team and ultimately can have a tremendous influence on the institution and how open it is to having Asian Americans work and thrive within it.

If we return to the stereotype content model, which is based on the two axes of warmth and competence, and reassess the image of Asian Americans, it's clear that they fall in an ambivalent quadrant, the one that embraces the judgments of competent but cold (see Table 5.1). Susan Fiske looks more closely at this stereotype in an article published in the *Annals of the American Academy of Political and Social Science* in 2012, titled "Managing Ambivalent Prejudices: Smart-but-Cold and Warm-but-Dumb Stereotypes." In it she concludes that people who fall in the "competent but cold" quadrants are typically viewed with ambivalence.

They are seen positively as competent, meaning bright and intelligent, but also as cold, an unfriendly category. Asian Americans typically fall in this quadrant. The groups that fall in this quadrant, including Jews and the rich (see Table 5.1), are often "out-groups" who face racism and anti-immigrant biases. Fiske also finds that the qualities of warmth and trust are more important in management than sheer status and power. In other words, people can more easily wield power after they gain trust, and so when it comes to the values preferred in the corporate world, trust takes precedence over competence.

Amy Cuddy, who for more than fifteen years has worked with Susan Fiske and Peter Glick on the stereotype content model, noted in her 2015 book *Presence* that when people first meet an individual or members of a group, whether in an office or in a dark alley, the goal is to determine quickly whether the strangers are friend or foe. And she notes that warmth and thus trustworthiness are the more important of the two dimensions.

This judgment has deep roots in our evolutionary history and is crucial for our survival. It's not that we don't value competent people, but we notice their competence only after we have judged their trustworthiness. When it comes to hiring and promoting people, corporation executives have plenty of competent people to choose from and so they want only those who are trustworthy. If a person is trustworthy, a friend, and competent, that person may be really useful in an organization. If a person is not trustworthy and a foe, especially if competent, that person may be very dangerous.

In corporate settings, executives and other employees may encounter people of different races or immigrant groups, and common stereotypes or biases often place those of different races or immigrant groups in so-called out-groups. Out-groups tend to be foes rather than friends. And stereotypes or implicit bias against Asian Americans could easily place them in an out-group. Asian Americans are stereotyped as capable and thus competent, but in the stereotype content model quadrant in which they fall, they are perceived as less warm and less social, which means they are closer to being a foe and in any case less trustworthy. This makes Asian Americans seem as competent foes who come across more as threats than as friends.

Asian Americans who are competent and cold can also be seen as targets of envy and resentment. Their coworkers may connect with them because they are capable, but they may also undermine them if they can get away with it. And realistically, do Asian Americans have the means to exert power in the corporate workplace? Or do white executives still have more power? And do the answers to these questions help explain why so few Asian Americans can be found in corporate leadership?

Many people would argue against this conclusion. As frequently noted, Asian Americans are viewed as the model minority. If we are placing a heavy burden on stereotypes, then Asian Americans clearly benefit from being regarded as the model minority. At the same time psychologists such as Hilary Bergsieker, Lisa Leslie, Vanessa Constantine, and Susan Fiske, using the stereotype content model in 2012, found that people stereotype others by omission. They tend to accentuate the positive and eliminate the negative. People want to tell the truth, and if there is an inconvenient fact, they may simply omit it. Thus it may seem that people have a very positive image of Asian Americans, while at the same time we hear little about how they are envied, resented, and not trusted.

Forever Foreign: Asians as Spies

The people I interviewed are all socially indistinguishable from American-born Asians. They are the native-born and members of the 1.5 generation—that is, they arrived in the United States before the age of thirteen. However, one image that is prevalent is that Asian Americans in general, including the people I interviewed, are perceived as "perpetual foreigners" or "forever foreign," a phrase coined by Mia Tuan in her 1999 book, *Forever Foreigners or Honorary Whites? The Asian Ethnic Experience Today.*

This image portrays Asian Americans as not being fully accepted by mainstream America, regardless of whether or not they were born in the United States or how long their parents have lived here. American-born individuals frequently conflate wrongdoing by foreign Asians with the wrongdoing of Asian Americans. Asian Americans who have been affected by these misperceptions have faced dire consequences, including loss of jobs and imprisonment.[8] In a 2016 *Slate* article titled "Just the Wrong Amount of American," Lowen Liu summarizes the tragic 1999 case of Wen Ho Lee, a Taiwanese American scientist who was wrongly accused of giving nuclear secrets to China in the mid 1980s but was supposedly not discovered by the FBI until 1995.[9] Despite the fact that Asian Americans rank high according to such measures as status, wealth, and education, they continue to be marginalized and continue to be victims of racism.

In particular, this image of Asian Americans as foreigners, as members of an out-group, has an impact when it comes to trust. Corporate employees are exposed to stereotypical images of Asian Americans as forever foreign, wealthy invaders, wartime enemies, and spies.[10] These images reinforce an image of an untrustworthy Asian American employee by pointing to wrongdoing by US citizens and noncitizens. In April 2019 the Trump administration rescinded visas for Chinese businessmen who were accused of being spies, even though they regularly traveled back and forth between Asia and America for work. The FBI has been flagging down Chinese-born scientists accusing them of violating rules and laws. As recently as May 2019, Chinese American professors were dismissed from Emory.[11] While there are seemingly positive stereotypes such as the model minority—the image of the hardworking, smart, dutiful Asian American that can reinforce the image of competent Asian

Americans—the more influential stereotype may be the more negative one, that of the untrustworthy Asian American.

The "forever foreign" stereotype ultimately affects all Asian Americans and is at work every time someone asks them "What country are you from?" or says "You speak English so well" or "Go back home."

In my study, only respondents at the highest levels reported that trust is the most important characteristic required at the executive levels, and very few on the lower rungs even mentioned the issue of trust. Yet clearly trust is relevant not only on the highest levels but also at the lowest levels. Trust involved meeting people, acting consistently over time, and having social skills (that is, being authentic, making eye contact, and spending more time with coworkers). Asian Americans have to focus on these skills with a clear aim to build trust. This includes making connections and networking that will help a person ascend beyond the midcareer level—from the first day on the job and even earlier.

The experiences described by the people I interviewed indicate that Asian Americans can focus on so-called soft skills by themselves and by finding mentors and sponsors. Asian Americans can practice these skills in their spare time or through professional or specific Asian American professional organizations. They can seek access to mentors, sponsors, and coaches. And of course, like many of those who made it to the C-suites, they had access to diversity and affirmative action programs such as the SEO Scholars, Posse, and Prep for Prep and later executive training programs at their own corporations. Every one of these programs taught them valuable social skills that aided their ascension to the C-suites.

As all this evidence shows, while specific professional and technical skills are generally seen as critical to a person becoming an occupant of a C-suite, far more essential is to learn how to build trust, which is rarely discussed in Asian American households and perhaps more important never mentioned in the playbook. And until that situation changes, it will continue to be difficult for ambitious Asian Americans to ascend to the higher levels of corporate America, despite their considerable skills in other areas.

6

The Double Bind for Asian American Women

I needed to push back and just could not rein myself in because
I'm not the demure type. Being assertive, but respectful helped
me maintain my standing among the men who were on the trading floor, but quite frankly it shocked those who were above me.

—Rickie, a Chinese American who received an MBA in the 1990s

AT first glance, Asian American women seem to be faring better in the corporate workplace than their Asian American male counterparts, if only because they earn more than white women thanks to the hyperselectivity of many of their immigrant parents and to their own high levels of education.[1] According to the US Bureau of Labor Statistics, the median weekly full-time earnings for Asian American women were $903, as compared to $770 for white women.[2] There's still a wage gap, though; Asian American women working full-time and year-round still earn only seventy-six cents for every dollar that Asian American men do.[3]

What's surprising is when it comes to landing coveted management positions in corporate America, Asian American women are the least likely of these four groups (i.e., Asian American men and women, and white men and women) to be successful.[4]

They are held back because of three different issues. The first involves the way Asian American women are brought up and the values they learned at home. More specifically, just like the playbook, it's not a product from Asia, but the way women are brought up is a mix of cultural values interacting and responding to the opportunity that is available in the United States. The second involves the way Asian American women are perceived in the workplace, including their role as a mother and the

147

effort it takes to balance both roles. These notions are externally situated. Finally, the third involves the issue of sexual harassment and the way it can further hamper Asian American women as they seek to make their way up the career ladder, in some instances affecting them more than it does white women because they are often isolated by race and gender. Asian American women have few allies who can help them through sexual/gender harassment when it arises.

All these factors have to be viewed using a framework of intersectionality.[5] Many of the Asian American women I interviewed made it clear that their professional options were limited not just by the bamboo ceiling, which Asian American men also face, or the glass ceiling, which limits the options of white women. They say they are doubly disadvantaged because of the prejudice born from the intersection of race and gender and the way that intersection produces structural obstacles for Asian American women.

Increasingly, the term "intersectionality" is being used to describe what it is like to be a member of two groups that suffer from discrimination. In this case, Asian American women are both women and Asian American and suffer bias when it comes to employment, thus creating barriers to promotion. Authors such as Penn State sociologist Emily Greenman and University of Michigan sociologist Yu Xie, in a 2008 article titled "Double Jeopardy?," published in *Social Forces*, have tried to determine how these biases operate in tandem. They argued that race and gender cannot be analyzed in isolation, an issue that all future research needs to take into account.

What's an Asian American Woman?

Asian American women have internalized many of the tenets of the playbook because being obedient, respectful, and compliant and listening to adults are behaviors that are valued at home just as they are at school. What's different is that, depending on birth order and whether they have brothers, women take on different responsibilities.

Angie Chung, a sociologist at SUNY Albany, explores this issue in her 2016 book, *Saving Face: The Emotional Costs of the Asian Immigrant Family Myth*. Chung discusses how the second-generation Asian American woman tries to renegotiate some of these terms in her relationship with her parents. And UCLA sociologist Min Zhou and Tulane University sociologist Carl Bankston, in their article "Family Pressure and the Educational Experience of the Daughters of Vietnamese Refugees," published in 2001 in *International Migration*, argue that Asian American parents' emphasis on education even for girls is really just an assertion of patriarchy in a new setting. Here in the United States, educated daughters are actually more valuable.

In addition, American culture has long been threaded with negative images of Asian or Asian American women, among them the doomed romantic female left by her American lover who is the title character of Puccini's 1904 opera *Madama Butterfly*, remade into the story of *Miss Saigon* in the character of Kim.[6]

More figures include the tiger mom, Yale Law School professor Amy Chua, who made a reputation for herself with her 2011 book about the rigor with which she raised her children; the manipulative "dragon lady," Imelda Marcos, the former first lady of the Philippines, admired for her beauty but also despised for her wasteful and lavish spending on herself; the China doll, a term that has come to signify a woman who is both beautiful and innocent; the quiet and demure lotus blossom; the sexy prostitute Suzie Wong, title character of the book and movie that bear her name; the edgy, even transgressive stand-up comedians and actresses Ali Wong and Margaret Cho; and of course the smart and industrious members of the model minority.[7] The intelligent, hardworking member of the model minority would be sought by corporate America. But do any of the other images reflect qualities needed to be a corporate leader? The answer is emphatically no.

The intense and demanding tiger mom and the manipulative and calculating dragon lady are far too overbearing to be regarded as desirable work colleagues. And characters who fall at the other end of the spectrum, such as the demure, acquiescent, and sexualized lotus flower, the geisha girl, and other compliant figures, are regarded as undesirable work colleagues for just the opposite reason. In one case Asian American women are regarded as too strong; in the other they are seen as not strong enough.

These stereotypes have real and often detrimental consequences when it comes to Asian American women moving ahead in corporate America. Writer-activist Sharon Chang, in her 2015 article in *Racism Review* titled "Searching for Women of Color," found that the term "Asian women," when searched on the Internet, appeared most often in advertisements about sex, dating, and marriage. Very few of the references referred to these women as leaders or as possessing leadership characteristics.

These biases not only affect who can lead corporations and ascend into the C-suites but also may be influential when it comes to the issue of sexual harassment, which produces a toxic work environment and affects a woman's ascendance to higher positions. While little research has been done on Asian American women in the workplace, even less research exists on the specific issue of Asian American women and sexual harassment on the job.

But as we know from testimony by such Asian American women as Ellen Pao, the former chief executive officer of the website Reddit who may be best known for the lawsuit she filed in 2012 charging her employer, the venture capital firm Kleiner Perkins, with gender discrimination and sexual harassment, Asian American women are harassed and taken advantage of in the workplace as much as or more than other women.[8] As part of the recent #MeToo movement, Asian American women in the technology industry have made a concerted effort to call attention to the harassment they face, but in most other fields, such as law, finance, and communications, these women have been unwilling to come forward and tell their stories.[9]

Research conducted by University of Kansas sociologists Chang-Hwan Kim and Yang Zhao, in their 2014 article "Are Asian American

Women Advantaged? Labor Market Performance of College Educated Female Workers" in *Social Forces*, showed that all Asian American women, regardless of education, are disadvantaged in at least one of the following areas when compared to white women: unemployment, annual earnings, and the number of people supervised in the workplace. In fact, even native-born Asian American women have no advantage when it comes to ascendancy in corporate America. They are less likely than white women to attain positions that involve supervision of other employees and more likely than white women to be unemployed. They do, however, earn just as much as and in some cases even more than white women because they live in areas with the highest cost of living.

And the 2017 ASCEND study that analyzed workforce data from Bay Area technology companies that had been compiled by the federal Equal Employment Opportunity Commission found that Asian American women were the least likely of all groups to become corporate executives.[10] In fact, Asian American white-collar professionals of both sexes are the least likely racial group, including blacks and Hispanics, to be promoted to be managers and executives.

In 2017, Yale Law School used data analysis, focus groups, and a national survey to produce a report that concluded that Asian American women are more likely to report experiencing discrimination on the basis of race than Asian American men. Moreover, while for nearly two decades Asian Americans have been the largest minority group in major law firms as associates, they also have had the highest attrition rates and represent the fewest number of partners.[11]

Parenthood and Achieving Work-Life Balance

Some Asian American women remove themselves from the executive pipeline because, like white women, they often have trouble balancing work and family demands. Family members, including parents and boyfriends or husbands, often pressure these women to spend more time at home and, once a couple has a child, to be a stay-at-home parent at least until a child is in school.

Even when Asian American women are young, especially if they are the children of immigrants, some are required to assume more in the way of household duties or responsibilities to the family because in male-dominated Asian culture it is assumed that women will automatically do such tasks.[12] Some of the women I interviewed mentioned, for example, that their brothers had fewer home responsibilities than they did.[13]

In addition, many of the young women I interviewed reported that they felt pressure from their parents, in-laws, and other relatives to settle down and marry, pressure that their brothers and other male relatives did not face. As a result, these women typically had children when they were in their late twenties or early thirties, and they reported that the resulting extra responsibility at home slowed or even halted their upward trajectory at work.

The women I interviewed often complained that they didn't realize that their parents, boyfriends, or husbands were so traditional in this respect. In fact, for most of these women's lives, their parents had expected them to do well in school and reveled in reaping the rewards gleaned from a daughter's prestigious and lucrative job.

However, when these women reached their late twenties and early thirties, their parents and partners started pressuring them to settle down and start a family, pressure that sometimes felt like an unexpected slap in the face. "My parents never said anything about having children," one woman reported, "but once they started discussing it, they would not stop."

Women from India and other South Asian countries often face this pressure with a twist. According to one South Asian American woman (who works in finance in New York City) I interviewed, some parents, as part of what they regard as their "obligation" to their South Asian American daughters, offered to find suitable partners by setting up an arranged marriage. According to this woman's parents, this would allow her to continue working without losing any time from work to date. Unsurprisingly, the woman declined the offer.

Even some women with East Asian parents faced this problem. Typical was a thirty-year-old Korean American management consultant named Eden, who had a degree from a small private college and was doing well in her career. Just a year earlier she had married another Korean American. Much to her surprise, shortly after her marriage her mother urged her to work less, travel less, and think about having children. Her mother-in-law echoed these suggestions. And both the mother and the mother-in-law raised these issues with her husband.

Eden was stunned by this turn of events, largely because her whole life had been focused on success in school and the workplace. She had never felt in a rush to be a parent. In fact, even as a child she recalled her parents telling her that she shouldn't have boyfriends because they would be too distracting and interfere with her performance in school, advice they repeated even once she started college.

Why the about-face? Part of the answer has to do with the ticking of a woman's biological clock, along with patriarchal notions as to which parent should work outside the home, and who should take care of children. Among Asian American families, there endures a strong sense that men should work outside the home and women should take care of children, whether or not they work outside the home. The belief in traditional sex roles was especially powerful among the Asian American professionals I interviewed.

When I asked about their own mothers, many of the women reported that their fathers earned enough money to allow their mothers to stay at home to raise them. This is no surprise, since most of the people I interviewed were the children of college-educated immigrants. Among this group, the fathers were often doctors, engineers, and professors. Even though their mothers did not hold jobs outside the home, the women I interviewed grew up in families that supported a woman's right to education and to work outside the home. Most of them had very supportive families who encouraged them to work and to move up the career ladder.

The women I interviewed had done very well in school and especially in their first jobs after college. Many of their stay-at-home mothers were praised for how well they had raised their daughters. However, as if a self-fulfilling prophecy were at work, the families reinforced the belief that the mother was the best person to raise the children, and if the mother wasn't available, the grandmother was the second-best person. Many parents assured their daughters that they had nothing to worry about when it came to combining career and family because they were available to take care of their grandchildren so that the daughter could focus on work.

Sometimes, however, spouses, parents, and in-laws demanded that a woman take time off from work to care for her children. Many of the women I interviewed mentioned this constraint. And only a few of them took their parents up on their offer of child care over the long term.

The Immigrant Bargain Comes Full Circle

Parental offers to help daughters with child care reflect another critical issue at work when it comes to determining how Asian American women fare in corporate America. This issue has to do with the so-called immigrant bargain, a powerful and enduring narrative that affects not only Asian Americans but most immigrant groups. This bargain acknowledges the fact that those who made the journey to America did so despite considerable hardship so that their children could enjoy a better life. In return, the children are expected to repay their parents for their sacrifices by getting a good education and flourishing in the workplace so as to reassure the older generation that their sacrifices were not in vain.

Offers of child care and similar assistance reflect the fact that the so-called immigrant bargain goes full circle. In immigration literature, the immigrant bargain is usually referred to as the obligation that the second generation feels toward their parents. The children owe the parents a great deal because the parents gave up so much to come here to provide opportunity for the children.

When a daughter or son has a child, the immigrant bargain can also be invoked, but in a parallel fashion. This time it is the parents who feel the obligation: they owe their children, especially their daughters, their assistance. Several of the women I interviewed told me that their immigrant parents were the sole caregivers of their grandchildren. That is because the parents are grateful that their children are doing well and will do whatever necessary to care for their grandchildren as long as their daughter has to work and does well for the whole three-generation "family." Among my respondents, if the grandparents took care of the grandkids, it was usually the daughters' mothers who felt obliged to ensure that their own daughter would move up in the work world.

As mentioned, this pattern of reciprocity, at least between the first-generation parents and the young second generation, is not limited to Asian Americans; it can be found among other immigrant groups as well. Robert Smith, author of the 2006 book *Mexican New York: Transnational Lives of New Immigrants*, and Vivian Louie, author of the 2012 book *Keeping the Immigrant Bargain: The Costs and Rewards of Success in America*, are sociologists who have studied intergenerational relations among Latinx families in order to explore what the immigrant bargain entails for them. Specifically, they analyzed how the bargain is seen as a transactional relationship between immigrant parents and their children. But they have yet to determine if the Latinx groups also see grandparents obliged to help their children in the care of the grandkids.

The women I interviewed underscored the fact that the immigrant bargain came full circle when they became adults. The immigrant bargain is full of obligations, originally owed by children to their parents, but parents in turn feel obligated to ensure the success of their children, especially their daughters. Parents were the ones who helped them through high school, helped them get into college, and paid for their tuition. They want to see the fruits of that labor. They want to ensure that the daughter can continue to work doubly hard to try to move up at work, and in some cases that also meant providing child care for the grandchildren.

While the Asian American women I interviewed did their best to excel in school, do well in college, and get a good job, life typically took a 180-degree turn when children arrived. My interviewees frequently referred to their parents as helpers. They said their parents felt obligated to help when they could.

In this transactional arrangement, it is the parents who now feel grateful for how much their children have accomplished, rather than vice versa. From the outside looking in, it appears that the children are still working the hardest, but they are no longer doing it for their parents' sake. They are now working hard, getting promoted, and earning more money to support themselves and their young families.

One woman I interviewed, who came from a working-class background, told me that she wanted to be able to buy a house for her parents.[14] As one formerly working-class respondent put it, "My parents worked for so long hoping that I can give them some security; I can at least make them feel secure." For these offspring, security in the United States is part of the immigrant bargain. And, she added, that security for her parents also involved making sure that their own grandchildren were taken care of.

These interviews with my respondents show that the immigrant bargain has been extended to include the parents doing what they can to ensure their children's and particularly their daughters' success in the work world. As we have seen, Asian American parents and extended family members often brag about their children's accomplishments and in the future envision bragging about their grandchildren's accomplishments.

Many of the women with children mentioned that their parents stepped in to take care of the grandchildren, at least for a short time. Lynn, a Korean American lawyer who rose to become senior counsel at her firm, was an Ivy League graduate who didn't expect her parents to cut back on their own activities to help her with their new grandchild. But, she told me, her parents really wanted to help out after she gave birth.

"With a new baby, my parents didn't think anyone, especially a stranger, could be a caring babysitter," she said. "They felt that a tiny baby couldn't complain, and he would be vulnerable. Plus, they wanted to help me out. Not only was it better for the baby, but they convinced me that they could accommodate my schedule better than a babysitter. My parents were always proud of me for being such a good girl so I think it's only natural that my mother would help me."

Family Balance at Work

Whether or not their parents helped with child care, Asian American women incurred more of a penalty than white women when it came to balancing work and family responsibilities because of the double bind in expectations as to how hard an Asian American is supposed to work and the image of the Asian American tiger mom, that is, a parent who will set extremely high standards for a child's behavior and accomplishments and make sure that these standards are met. For this reason, at least half of the women I interviewed reported that returning to work after having a child proved extremely difficult.

Some of the women I interviewed returned from maternity leave to face relentless schedules in the office. Some of the women left work again for a time when their children were in elementary or middle school. In both cases, when they returned to work they often had to refashion and upgrade their skills because of the fast-changing nature of the corporate workplace. This of course slowed their ascent in the corporate world.

As happens with women of every group, many of them found that when they returned to work their progress was impeded or they were relegated to the so-called mommy track. Some who returned after an especially long maternity leave had a harder time returning to the positions they once held. One respondent, a 1990s college graduate, was going to try for a Goldman Sachs "returnship," akin to an internship but for those who had left work for more than a couple of years.[15]

The double burden of work and parenting proved too much for some. "My parents and my husband thought that I needed to spend more time at home with the kids, so I relented," one woman told me. "I took time off when they were in elementary school. Thus began my second leave."

As we have seen, Asian Americans typically feel that they must work extra hard to prove themselves "worthy" of being promoted. This bias continues when a woman becomes a new mother. Upon the return to work, many saw their careers slow down. Still others realized that they were set up for failure.

A few of the women told me that they were expected to be able to handle the already excessive workload they had shouldered before maternity leave and to be even more aggressive after their return. The stereotype of the robotic Asian workaholic seemed to haunt them. Women who were already in management were given even more demanding projects with more people to oversee.

"They think I'm devoted to work, and they expect me to do that much more," a Korean American lawyer said. "It's an unfair expectation. And unfortunately, I feel responsible that if I can't do it, all these other Asian American women won't be given a chance." As many others have pointed out, among them Joan C. Williams and Rachel Dempsey in their 2014 book, *What Works for Women at Work: Four Patterns Working Women Need to Know*, this double bind reinforces stereotypes and makes it even harder for women to return to work, let alone try to get promoted.

There are other images that have a gendered effect. Shelley Correll (2007), a professor of sociology at Stanford, has written extensively about the "motherhood penalty" and the "fatherhood bonus," but these categories grow especially complicated when the issue of race is introduced as consequence of intersectionality. As a Chinese American lawyer named Angie told me, "There were all these stereotypes of me being a tiger mom. My coworkers thought I was taking all this time to parent from work. They had these misconceptions of me that only stereotyped me as an overwrought mom who couldn't concentrate on work and was obsessed with raising hypercompetitive kids. So not only was I on the 'mommy track' but I was on the 'tiger mommy track.'"

As a result of these attitudes, Angie said, she was self-conscious whenever people asked her about her children. Her coworkers, most of them white males, made her uncomfortable. As has long been the case, men were considered heroic if they took a child to soccer practice, but women were discouraged from speaking about their children in the workplace or even having pictures of their children on their desk. Asian American women faced special backlash when they had children because it was assumed that they were so hardworking and hard driving that there was more pressure to put the demands of their job ahead of the demands of their family.

In their book *What Works for Women at Work* Williams and Dempsey also point out that the stereotype of Asian American women as hardworking and devoted to their jobs conflicts with the stereotype that they are also family oriented, and this juxtaposition of images creates conflicts at work that do not operate in her favor. While companies reap a great deal by having such a woman in their employ, while they value her abilities, unless she occupies a C-suite or is close to doing so, most coworkers typically wonder what she is doing at the office. And if she does mention her children, she is more likely to face a backlash.

Intersectionality and the #MeToo Movement

Asian American mothers are not the only Asian American women to face problems in the workplace. Intersectionality in the office also affects Asian American women without children. The best-known example of this is Ellen Pao, a Chinese American, an American-born Asian.

In the past two years, the rise of the #MeToo movement has encouraged women, especially in the field of entertainment, to share their experiences involving sexual harassment and assault.[16] Tarana Burke, the originator of the movement, in 2006 encouraged using the phrase "MeToo" to encourage "empowerment through empathy" among women of color.[17] And during the period that the current #MeToo movement emerged, a number of the women I had interviewed in previous years contacted me again, this time to discuss how they had been affected by sexual harassment in the workplace.

Previously, only one woman had raised this issue. She had been un-officially blackballed from the finance industry after filing a lawsuit in which she contended that she had been sexually harassed in the work-place. As venture capitalist Maha Ibrahim was quoted as saying in a 2017 article in *USA Today*, bringing up the issue of sexual harassment was like "dropping a nuclear bomb on your career."[18]

Although a high-ranking woman like Pao is not the person people usually think of when they think about discrimination against Asian Americans in the workplace, her lawsuit against her employer is gener-ally described as an action involving both gender discrimination and sexual harassment. Pao was one of the very few Asian American women at the top in the field of technology, and her lawsuit against her em-ployer, Kleiner Perkins, and her fraught resignation from Reddit reveal both hidden and overt biases against Asian American women in leader-ship positions.[19]

In her 2017 book *Reset: My Fight for Inclusion and Lasting Change*,[20] Pao describes an experience she had early on in her career at Kleiner Perkins that underscores the impact of intersectionality. Pao tried to explain to her employer that racism or at least implicit bias existed at her workplace and in particular that not all Asian American women looked alike. According to her, the company's chief executive officer, John Doerr, claimed not to be able to tell his female Asian American employees apart, even when they were his chief of staff.

Pao poked fun at his weakness during a holiday party where she in-terchanged PowerPoint slides of his former chief of staff, Aileen Lee, an Asian American female wearing no glasses, with her own photo, in which she was wearing glasses. Everyone enjoyed the stunt, but the next day Doerr reverted to calling Pao Aileen. As Pao summed up his behav-ior, "We have a long way to go, as women and minorities continue to make up a small fraction of the management at our most lucrative and productive companies."

Pao's experience is especially important because her story involves not just racism but also sexism and sexual harassment, all of which limited her movement up the career ladder.[21] However, in part because of Pao, the visibility of her lawsuit, and other public testimony of Asian American women in recent years, the women I interviewed were increasingly comfortable confiding in me about sexual harassment in the fields of finance, media, law, insurance, and creative technology.

Sexual Harassment

When I first started to conduct interviews for this study, only one woman, a Chinese American named Sue who was a 1980s Ivy League graduate, was willing to confess that she had been a victim of sexual harassment in the workplace. Sue was a vice president in a finance firm, and while she is still employed, she no longer works in that field. Once she filed a complaint of sexual harassment against a managing director, she received barely any raises and was promoted only once. When she finally left the firm, she was never again hired by another finance firm. Her experience was especially disquieting since it seemed to be a signal that other such victims were penalized if they spoke up.

Other women respondents told me that they were unwilling to say anything about sexual harassment in the workplace because it was the norm and because their careers would stall if such behavior were exposed. To keep their jobs, they told me, they would simply have to learn to deal with men who behaved badly.

It was easy to believe that sexual harassment was widespread among Asian American women, especially after reading articles about Asian American women in the technology industry who were willing to speak up about the issue after Ellen Pao's lawsuit.[22] But with few women of color in these industries being able to speak out forcefully without fear about damaging their careers, it's difficult to understand the full complexity of the situation.[23]

When Asian American women are targeted for sexual harassment, as Williams and Dempsey wrote, we see what is described as a "gendered power dynamic as well as a racial power dynamic." The authors describe two injuries. First there is a racial component, in which Asian American women may be seen as more sexually available than white women or more likely to submit to advances. This harkens to the stereotype of Asian American women as demure, quiet, and unlikely to complain. In addition, an Asian American woman may be the only such person in a leadership position in a company.

These factors make such a woman feel more vulnerable and encourage images of her as a perfect victim. Because of the stereotypes of Asian women, some may think they are actually inviting sexual attention. The men in turn may feel that these women are easy to have sex with and will not fight back or complain. These are ideal images for men who seek to harass or sexually abuse their Asian American coworkers.

The women I spoke with cited many ways that men at work asserted themselves sexually, ranging from making lewd comments and putting their hands on their lower back or thigh to brushing against their breasts and kissing and groping them. One woman said that on a few business trips a male coworker kept insisting on having sex with her.

And all of these women said that they had few places or people to turn to who would understand what they were experiencing. They did not feel comfortable speaking to women who were not Asian American because they knew that some of them also accepted the racist and sexist stereotypes of Asian American women as being easy sexual partners. Nor did they feel comfortable telling coworkers, knowing how quickly news travels in the workplace. One woman said she thought that she would get a better promotion if she did as the man said. All of these women, however, felt especially vulnerable as Asian American women and believed that their careers would be jeopardized if they spoke out.

Sue, the woman who had worked in finance, told me that she never expected that sexual harassment and its aftermath would be as horrible as it was. She endured groping, kissing, and more, but once she protested, the man retaliated by having her removed from lucrative projects and by making it difficult for her to get bonuses. When she filed her claim, she felt that she had evidence necessary to document his behavior, but the firm did not support her lawsuit.

Sue was one of only a few Asian American women in her firm, and during the 1980s, she said, it seemed as if "all women were being harassed, but it was worse for Asian American women." And she added, "The white women did not warn me against predators in the office. Of course they were white men, and I believe the white women believed the men were just harassing me because—that it was easy sex with us." What Sue was saying was that when it came to sexual harassment, Asian American women were easy targets. Although she complained to management, no one, not even white women, would support her claims.

Diversity and Affirmative Action Programs for Women

Given all the obstacles Asian American women face, what can they do to ensure that they maintain or increase their presence in the corporate world? One answer is programs that have been designed to increase diversity in the workplace. Programs that have helped women get corporate jobs have also helped Asian American women. The people who run these programs are well aware of the disparity in the numbers of women in all of the elite, specialized professional fields, including finance, media, law, insurance, and creative technology.

Most of the Asian American women I spoke to said they thought that they had been helped by diversity and affirmative action programs. Most of them said they thought that programs designed to help women were more important than those specifically designed to help Asian Americans. As Nira, an Indian American who had graduated from a small elite college in the 1990s, said, "Affirmative action programs for women are important because women don't have the advantages that men have. Programs need to look out for them and get them into these jobs. Men help each other out automatically. Look what happens in a meeting," she added. "They don't listen to us. They listen to each other. I really appreciate programs that look out for women."

Lynn, a Korean American woman who graduated from an Ivy League college in the 1980s and is an executive in the investment industry, agreed. Lynn is among the very few minority women at her level, and when she joined the company she works for, she was able to do so because she was part of a cohort of minorities who were introduced to the firm. She found a sponsor, an African American male who was willing to take on a group of minorities to help move them up in that workplace.

"These programs matter," Lynn said. "You get exposure. But then it's up to me/you to make use of the information they give you. It's not like there is a net to save you if you fall. But you do learn. And for people without connections to people who can teach you, these affirmative action programs for women and minorities are the best we can do." Moreover, programs such as the returnship focus on women with proven skills who just need to update their skills.[24]

When it comes to breaking through the bamboo ceiling, Asian American women still have a long way to go. Many obstacles stand in their way. However, they are coming to realize that such programs are necessary. Whatever name one gives them, the programs themselves are essential to counter racial and sexual discrimination.

Although some people claim that the concept of intersectionality is sometimes used as an excuse to explain certain prejudice and discrimination, given the stereotypes that adhere to Asian American women,[25] it seems as if they are particularly vulnerable to both discrimination in the workplace and sexual harassment in a way that Asian American men or women of other ethnicities might not be, in that the stereotypes for both groups—women and Asian Americans—are exactly the opposite of what the American corporate workplace seeks when it comes to promotion and because both stereotypes feed into the idea of individuals who are likely targets of sexual harassment.

In other words, if women in general are seen as not fit for corporate promotion and likely targets for sexual harassment, Asian American women, who may be perceived both as weak and as playthings, are especially vulnerable. The two stereotypes echo and reinforce each other.

Conclusion

Reworking the Playbook

As I conclude this book, in the fall of 2019, I am writing in a world that is changing in profound ways and with breathtaking speed, sometimes for the better, far more often for the worse.

On the one hand, great strides are being made when it comes to understanding and accepting the diversity and complexity of American culture and the many groups it comprises. We are benefiting from a more open and tolerant society, one that increasingly embraces people with disabilities and mental illnesses. There's an increasingly greater tolerance for mixed-race relationships. When it comes to attitudes toward members of the LGBTQ community—people who are lesbian, gay, bisexual, transgender, and queer—both laws and public attitudes have shifted with what many consider extraordinary speed. The celebration in the summer of 2019 of Gay Pride Month, marking the fiftieth anniversary of the police raid on Stonewall, the now legendary gay bar in Greenwich Village that is widely considered the birthplace of the contemporary gay rights movement, was a dramatic sign of the times.

And thanks to the #MeToo movement, which, starting in the fall of 2017, largely through a series of powerful articles in the *New York Times* and the *New Yorker*, brought extraordinary attention to female victims of often violent sexual harassment in the workplace, within the last few years there has been a dramatic shift in an understanding of the ways that women, especially African American women, have suffered from decades of sexual harassment and assault in the workplace. There is hardly an area of American life, from politics to entertainment, from media to medicine, from sports to academia, from the military to the arts, from manufacturing to finance, from government to law, that has not been touched and in some cases transformed by the escalating number of women who have spoken up about the abuse and in many cases the emotional and physical violence they have suffered, some of it going back many decades.

But when it comes to the issue of race and ethnicity, the picture is far murkier and the progress far more halting. While changes in attitudes have occurred in recent decades, sparked in part by the 2008 election of Barack Obama, the nation's first African American president, that transformation has been sputtering and in a growing number of cases has been marked by lethal violence. Despite decades worth of civil rights legislation, lawsuits, and affirmative action programs that have profoundly reshaped so many areas of American life, incidents involving discrimination, abuse, and deep-seated hostility to people of different races and ethnic groups seem to be an almost daily occurrence.

One dramatic example of this is the escalating number of charges of police brutality against young men of color around the country. Another is the so-called Muslim ban that President Donald Trump tried to institute in early 2017 in an effort to bar people from Muslim-majority countries from entering the United States. Still another is President Trump's comment about "very fine people on both sides" after a white supremacist, neo-Nazi rally at the University of Virginia in 2017. The number of anti-Semitic attacks in the United States has also escalated, as has been the case around the world, and in some cases these attacks have resulted in lethal violence—for example, the 2018 fatal shooting at a synagogue in Pittsburgh, in which eleven people were killed, making it the deadliest attack on a Jewish community in the nation.

There is no way of knowing how Asian Americans and other nonwhites will fare in this highly politicized and racialized environment, one in which emotions seem to be running at a higher pitch by the day. Americans are currently in the midst of figuring out how to define a multiracial democracy, and for a variety of complicated reasons the process is incredibly painful on many fronts.

* * *

As I write, in the fall of 2019, many Americans are still reeling from President Trump's Twitter attack earlier in the year on four progressive Democratic congresswomen of color—Alexandria Ocasio-Cortez (NY), Ilhan Omar (MN), Ayanna Pressley (MA), and Rashida Tlaib (MI)—directing them to "go back" to their "corrupt" and "broken and crime infested" places from which they came before "telling the people of the United States . . . how our government is to be run." At a subsequent rally in North Carolina during which the president attacked each congresswoman individually, when he mentioned Omar, the crowd started chanting, "Send her back!" an echo of the president's tweet demanding that she be deported. Omar, a naturalized American citizen, had come to the United States as a refugee from Somalia when she was a child. The other three congresswomen the president attacked were all born in the United States.[1]

The president's attacks came hard on the heels of cascading revelations that Latin American migrants crossing the border from Mexico, among them young children and even toddlers, have been separated from their parents and sequestered in quarters so punishing and degrading that some observers have likened them to internment and even concentration camps.

Immigrants, including second-generation Asian Americans and members of many other groups, also feel the sting of the "go back home" comments that President Trump aimed at the four congresswomen.[2] For decades, indeed for centuries, it has been an implicit question as to whether nonwhites who have been a part of the United States, whether by immigration, slavery, or native birth, are truly part of the fabric of our country. Having Asian Americans on the executive team of large corporations is one sign that members of this group are finally a part of this society. But the reality is that there are very few Asian Americans who head these organizations. And while there may seem to be little in common between the plight of suffering migrants and the professional aspirations of Ivy League professionals, there is no question that anti-immigrant attitudes prevalent in the culture can reach into unexpected crannies of society and affect attitudes in the most unlikely of places.

To try to better understand why Asian Americans struggle to reach the higher echelons of corporate life in America, I examined the double-edged implications of the "pull yourself up by your bootstraps" mentality so clearly repeated in the playbook that it is ingrained in the minds of the vast majority of second-generation Asian Americans. I also explored why a belief in this mantra can make it hard for young Asian Americans to recognize the critical importance of constricting racial attitudes in the corporate workplace and what they can do to change the situation.[3] Finally, I suggested a few concrete ways that Asian Americans can address the challenges of moving up in the corporate American workplace.

Race Matters

In many respects, at the root of the problem is the Asian American playbook, the orally delivered set of maxims and advice for success in school and beyond, to which all of my respondents referred and which many followed at least in part until they landed an entry-level job. The playbook exhorted them to follow a seemingly straight path that would lead them to realization of the American dream; they could "make it" on their own, they were taught, using individual effort to persuade others as to their competence or merit—the playbook's narrow definition of worthiness.

Many Asian Americans worked hard to get great grades and test scores in high school, became captains of swim, tennis, volleyball, robotics, computer science, and math teams, became editors of school newspapers, officers of student government, and leaders of other extracurricular activities, and received degrees from top colleges and graduate schools. Some even followed a path into the STEM fields, in which it is presumed that Asian Americans will do well. But the people I interviewed pursued careers in finance, media, law, insurance, and creative technology. They found entry-level jobs and many of them earned high incomes, yet the returns for their years of schooling were often less than the returns for their white coworkers. Many of these Asian Americans were able to move ahead but sometimes at a slower pace than they expected and frequently at a slower pace than their white colleagues.

As we have seen, only very few Asian Americans are given the opportunity to enter the executive suites. By examining a small but significant aspect of the professional work life of Asian Americans, my goal was to offer information and advice that will be helpful to Asian Americans in general.

What is clearly missing from the playbook is any realistic discussion of systemic discrimination and racism against Asian Americans, leaving some of the people I interviewed often unsure if they were even the victim of racism and if so how to respond to or correct the situation.[4] While many of my respondents have seen examples of racial discrimination directed toward their families, only a few cited examples in which they themselves were the victim of discrimination or racism. Rather, they most often discussed examples that they labeled implicit bias.

At the time of my interviews, between 2014 and 2016, most of the people I spoke to defined discrimination as an attitude that had long disappeared, at least for them. Rather, it was something that their parents, first-generation immigrants, had faced. But members of the second generation, who speak English without an accent and hold college degrees from elite and select institutions, believed that they should not face explicit racism. Yet they face implicit bias, which may be less horrific but nonetheless can have punishing if subtler effects.

Moreover, many of the people I interviewed made it clear that they were not prepared to deal with failure at the workplace because they didn't assume that such failure was often a result of prejudice. They thought failure was their own fault, despite the fact that they had put so much effort into getting to where they were and much of the time following the maxims of the playbook. In fact, if failure was their own fault, they concluded, it was up to them to work even harder to fix things.

Some of the people I interviewed seem to suggest that they see themselves "reading" as white and elite as opposed to black or Latinx. And because many of them are children of college-educated parents who live in mostly white neighborhoods and attended mostly white schools, many of them felt that they were not afflicted with the same kind of discrimination as that thrust upon blacks and Latinx.

Clearly, Asian Americans have for a variety of complex reasons been protected from some of the most horrific forms of racism. Some of my respondents believe this, and I also think that many whites, blacks, and Latinx may also read Asian Americans as white and thus may not support their claims as to the importance of race and the impact of racism. This may be part of the reason why many groups, minority or other, don't understand that Asian Americans might be subject to discrimination and hence eligible for help when it comes to combatting discrimination.

Ironically, when the Asian Americans I interviewed do come up against failure that can be traced to discrimination, they typically don't recognize it fully or maybe don't know how to react to it. For example, when one of the women I interviewed was told that she didn't "look the part" for a certain high-level job, she hired an executive coach to work on her dress and speech so that she would fit in better with the white majority at the company where she worked. When I mentioned this example to another interviewee, she replied, "Do you mean they are trying to tell her that she doesn't have the right hair?" One interviewee clearly thinks the comment is about learning the proper corporate dress for success etiquette; the other clearly thinks that the comment has to do with race and how a person has to deal with racism.[5]

Attitudes of the people I interviewed (and their employers) may also be influenced by recent events targeting minorities and especially Asian American academics as spies, as was clear from my discussion of the case of Wen Ho Lee and many others in his position.[6] Maybe Asian Americans will begin to see race and racism much more clearly, given the way that these Chinese academics, who are typically American citizens, have been treated.[7]

Finally, the playbook's narrow definition of worthiness as measured by hard work and merit, performing well, attaining high test scores, earning a graduate degree, and performing in exemplary fashion when it comes to projects at work needs to be expanded. For example, many people work hard by putting in long hours—a positive trait because they can improve a skill. However, even though putting in the hours is important, hard work alone is not the basis for success. And another example of how the playbook's maxims can be misleading and even harmful when it comes to ascending the executive ladder is that the playbook assumes that tests are fair measurements of hard skills. As a result, a young Asian American is unlikely to consider the fact that failure based on tests or hard skills may be due not to performance but to race.[8] This color-blind view of the world as a place that rewards individual effort is shared by the playbook. Thus, when many young Asian Americans are failing to achieve their goals, they often seek a color-blind solution that does not take into consideration society's structural problems but simply leaves them working harder.

Many of these Asian American respondents do not have the language to say, "One can't address racism without seeing race."[9] The proven solutions for addressing the problem of discrimination at the workplace are structural solutions that address race and include affirmative action programs. For example, Dobbin and Kalev found that recruitment, mentoring/sponsoring, and management training and management development programs are effective in corporations and lead to accountability, ensuring that women and minorities, including Asian Americans, move up in those organizations. Yet it is these types of race-conscious programs that have come under attack. This was very clear in the Harvard case.

The Harvard Case, Holistic Admissions, and Race-Conscious Admissions

Asian Americans have been at the center of the affirmative action debate at Harvard University. And as was true with the people I interviewed, there are Asian Americans on both sides of the issues.

The case involving Harvard hinged on the issue of whether Asian Americans are penalized by the university's admissions policies, which in an effort to create a diverse student body took race into consideration when deciding which applicants to admit. This case was argued in the fall of 2018 and ended with a second round of final arguments in February 2019. On October 1, 2019, the Massachusetts District Court ruled in favor of holistic and race-conscious admissions. The court declared that Harvard's affirmative action admissions process was working well and that in order to make minor improvements, the school could make an effort to remove implicit bias.

The university had argued that its race-conscious admissions programs benefit all students including Asian Americans.[10] Harvard lawyers and a group known as the Coalition for a Diverse Harvard, of which I am a founder, showed that the number of Asian American students at the university has steadily increased since 1980 (when affirmative action was in its early stages) to the point where the class of 2023 is over 25 percent Asian American.[11]

The university had been charged with bias against Asian American applicants. The plaintiffs, a group known as Students for Fair Admissions (SFFA), led by a politically conservative legal strategist named Edward Blum and some unnamed Asian American students who had been rejected by Harvard, contended that the relief should come in the form of the elimination of race-conscious admissions or affirmative action. This relief would target the process that benefits all students, not just Asian Americans.[12]

Following the playbook, SFFA and some Asian American parents and students believe that a color-blind approach to admissions will help Asian American students. They argue that by purporting to examine each student without taking race into consideration, the system is more fair.

Instead of recognizing Asian American students as authentic individuals with a racial background that influences who they are, whether by a lot or a little, members of this group want racial identity removed entirely from the admissions process. But without race as a factor in an admissions process that considers the whole person, not just academic achievement, how will students be able to share aspects of their lives that truly show who they are? Witnesses testifying on behalf of the university, including myself, showed that race can have a huge influence on the life trajectory of all students.[13] A goal of current affirmative action programs is to expose all students, majority and minority, to each other and thereby make them more tolerant and understanding of differences among individuals.

This is one of the crucial lessons from the C-suite executive respondents. Executives need to be trusted. To be trusted, a person has to be authentic, and being authentic includes being able to recognize one's race and its impact. Seventeen-year-olds can learn these lessons too. Moreover, what are the implications for the workplace if race-conscious admissions at the college level are removed? As I have shown, affirmative action is an effective program to increase diversity at the workplace.

The SHSAT Cases in New York City

The recent controversy surrounding New York City's Specialized High School Admissions Test, known as the SHSAT, shows how following the playbook, which places enormous emphasis on test scores, can adversely affect the children of the city's poor and working-class Asian Americans.

The dispute has to do with admissions to the New York City specialized high schools, a group that includes Stuyvesant, Bronx Science, Brooklyn Tech, and five other smaller high schools.[14] A group of Chinese American parents along with other parents became engaged in a campaign to keep the SHSAT as the only criterion for admittance into the eight specialized high schools. These parents, following the tenets in the playbook, believe that the admissions process is color-blind and that any child who works very hard can have a chance of getting into one of these schools.

However Asian American students make up 60 percent of the student body in specialized schools, while only 15 percent of the public school population is Asian American.[15] Meanwhile black and Latinx students make up 70 percent of the public school population while constituting only 10 percent of the students in the specialized high schools. To many, this looks like discrimination against black and Latinx students, and the elimination of the test is seen as one of the only ways to prevent this. Yet the Asian American population in New York City has the highest level of poverty of any group.

A group of parents including Chinese parents believe in the test— there is a whole industry of after school, summer, and weekend classes to help the children prepare for these tests. In the eyes of these parents, their children are working hard over many hours using these resources to prepare. These parents stress individual effort. Not all Chinese American parents nor all the people I interviewed agree that the test should be retained. Those who would prefer to eliminate the test believe that if the children's time were freed up from test preparation, they would be able to practice social skills and participate in other activities. Social skills in particular have been shown to be essential when it comes time for promotion up the career ladder.

Social Skills, Trust, and Race

Asian Americans who have made it to executive offices say they are trusted despite the fact that there are a whole set of stereotypes about Asian American employees, especially that the individual is "forever foreign" and can't be trusted. Over the history of Asian immigration, some of the tropes have been that they are wealthy invaders, academic threats, refugees, wartime enemies, spies, and tiger moms. Getting to know people other than members of their own group gives each Asian American multiple dimensions and challenges these stereotypes.

I believe that trust is a key issue and that it is important for Asian Americans to rethink how to build trust in light of the systemic racism and stereotypes still prevalent in American culture. Trust should be seen as something a person can work on starting at a young age. Clearly those who ascend to the top are all capable people, but one way of getting to the top is to have other people's backs, to believe in others and let others believe in you, to know when others can take a seat near you at the top, to know when they can protect you and the organization, largely because they also trust that you will have the capability to back up what you say given all of your talents. Trust is a social skill that needs to be included in the playbook tenets.

The playbook, while its tenets work when it comes to some areas of life, is clearly not complete. When it comes to making one's way in corporate America, there are many other important and even critical lessons to be learned. As I hope this book has shown, these few changes can have a profound effect on how Asian Americans fare in America's corporate workplace. The more quickly and effectively these lessons can be mastered, the greater the chances Asian Americans will have of breaking through to the C-suites and the more success and satisfaction they will reap during the journey, especially as we advocate for longer term structural changes. Lessons that may have served an earlier generation well need to be rethought and rewritten to serve the men and women who will come after. These vital shifts can impact future generations and enable Asian Americans to lift up the next cohort toward the top.

Acknowledgments

WRITING and researching this book over the past five years has meant that a variety of companions from all walks of my life helped sustain me. Producing a book is impossible without sufficient support of all manner. With a project that has taken so long to complete, there are many who are valuable to me but may not be named.

First of all, this book could not have come to fruition without all the Asian American professionals, executive coaches, and conference attendees who willingly spoke to me. Though they remain anonymous as I promised, I am ever grateful for their participation. In addition, I thank my colleagues who supported me intellectually in numerous ways including sharpening the initial project, sharing insights from chapter themes, giving feedback after presentations, and reading chapters. These include Syed Ali, Vivian Louie, Van Tran, Natasha Warikoo, Pawan Dhingra, Herb Gans, Phil Kasinitz, and Nancy Foner; grad students Hyein Lee and Philipp Sanbongi; and assistant Sheryl Quock. My own Hunter College and Graduate Center colleagues and especially my Sociology departments led by chairs Erica Chito Childs and Lynn Chancer deserve much thanks. Other scholars and people engaged in inequality have always been an inspiration. They include Nadia Kim, Oiyan Poon, Janelle Wong, Julie Park, Karthick Ramakrishnan, Jennifer Lee, the NAACP Legal Defense Fund team, the Lawyers Committee team, and the Advancing Justice Team, among many others.

Outside of academia, thanks to friends and family who share my many interests, keep me going and smiling—Jane, Jeannie, Kristin, Michael, Winnie, Annette, Alan, Kyle, Jade, Bob, Jennifer, Alan, and many more of my special gym, dancing, and/or dining friends. In gratitude to all who have kept me sane and encouraged during this process.

In the funding circle, I want to thank the academic community from the Advanced Research Collaborative (ARC) in 2017 for a semester without teaching, allowing me to analyze the data and to be with cheerful colleagues. Time off and monies were also awarded to me by the PSC-CUNY, Hunter College's Roosevelt House and the Presidential Research and Travel Funds.

Appendix

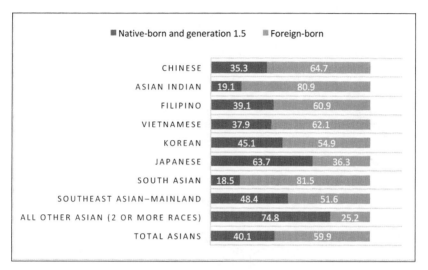

Figure A.1. Nativity Status (Percentages) by Asian American Ethnicity

Source: American Community Survey 2013–17 five-year PUMS.
Note: All Asian Americans ages 25–64 years and employed full-time in the profit and nonprofit sectors. South Asian includes Bhutanese, Nepalese, Bangladeshi, Pakistani, Sri Lankan. Southeast Asian–mainland includes Cambodian, Hmong, Laotian, Thai, Burmese, Indonesian, Malaysian.

Table A.1. Nativity Status by Sex, Separately by Asian American Ethnicity

Sex	Nativity status	Chinese	Asian Indian	Filipino	Vietnamese	Korean	Japanese	South Asian	Southeast Asian–mainland	All other Asians, including two or more races	Total
Males	Native and gen 1.5	272,818	165,109	245,474	136,848	122,162	96,492	30,080	103,314	398,669	1,570,966
		36.3%	16.8%	46.5%	39.4%	43.7%	63.6%	15.8%	49.0%	73.6%	39.4%
	Foreign-born	477,835	819,723	282,864	210,757	157,336	55,194	160,451	107,370	142,704	2,414,234
		63.7%	83.2%	53.5%	60.6%	56.3%	36.4%	84.2%	51.0%	26.4%	60.6%
	Total	750,653	984,832	528,338	347,605	279,498	151,686	190,531	210,684	541,373	3,985,200
		100.0%	100.0%	100.0%	100.0%	100.0%	100.0%	100.0%	100.0%	100.0%	100.0%
Females	Native and gen 1.5	229,447	123,647	204,265	113,729	113,242	79,632	19,450	89,583	335,423	1,308,418
		34.2%	23.6%	32.9%	36.3%	46.6%	63.8%	25.0%	47.7%	76.1%	40.9%
	Foreign-born	441,469	400,178	416,265	199,479	129,684	45,251	58,439	98,415	105,315	1,894,495
		65.8%	76.4%	67.1%	63.7%	53.4%	36.2%	75.0%	52.3%	23.9%	59.1%
	Total	670,916	523,825	620,530	313,208	242,926	124,883	77,889	187,998	440,738	3,202,913
		100.0%	100.0%	100.0%	100.0%	100.0%	100.0%	100.0%	100.0%	100.0%	100.0%
Total Employed Asians	Native and gen 1.5	502,265	288,756	449,739	250,577	235,404	176,124	49,530	192,897	734,092	2,879,384
		35.3%	19.1%	39.1%	37.9%	45.1%	63.7%	18.5%	48.4%	74.7%	40.1%
	Foreign-born	919,304	1,219,901	699,129	410,236	287,020	100,445	218,890	205,785	248,019	4,308,729
		64.7%	80.9%	60.9%	62.1%	54.9%	36.3%	81.5%	51.6%	25.3%	59.9%
	Total	1,421,569	1,508,657	1,148,868	660,813	522,424	276,569	268,420	398,682	982,111	7,188,113
		100.0%	100.0%	100.0%	100.0%	100.0%	100.0%	100.0%	100.0%	100.0%	100.0%

Source: American Community Survey 2013–17 five-year PUMS.   Note: All Asian Americans ages 25–64 years and employed full-time in the profit and nonprofit sectors.

Table A.2. Percentage in Age Group by Asian American Ethnicity for Only Native-Born and Generation 1.5

	25–34 years	35–44 years	45–54 years	55–64 years
Chinese	42.5%	30.4%	18.2%	8.9%
Asian Indian	52.7%	32.7%	11.9%	2.7%
Filipino	40.8%	32.7%	19.0%	7.4%
Vietnamese	45.1%	35.9%	17.7%	1.4%
Korean	45.2%	35.0%	16.4%	3.4%
Japanese	18.9%	20.7%	30.1%	30.3%
South Asian	61.3%	26.2%	9.9%	2.6%
Southeast Asian–mainland	53.1%	33.2%	12.0%	1.7%
All other Asians	43.3%	30.9%	17.7%	8.1%
Total Asians	43.5%	31.5%	17.5%	7.5%

Source: American Community Survey 2013–17 five-year PUMS.
Note: All Asian Americans ages 25–64 years and employed full-time in the profit and nonprofit sectors.

Table A.3. Nativity Status within Age Group by Asian American Ethnicity

Asian American ethnicity	Nativity status	25–34 years	35–44 years	45–54 years	55–64 years	Total
Chinese	Native and gen 1.5	53.8%	38.7%	23.5%	18.6%	35.3%
	Foreign-born	46.2%	61.3%	76.5%	81.4%	64.7%
Asian Indian	Native and gen 1.5	28.4%	18.0%	11.6%	5.0%	19.1%
	Foreign-born	71.6%	82.0%	88.4%	95.0%	80.9%
Filipino	Native and gen 1.5	67.3%	44.4%	27.3%	14.4%	39.1%
	Foreign-born	32.7%	55.6%	72.7%	85.6%	60.9%
Vietnamese	Native and gen 1.5	70.6%	44.0%	23.2%	3.3%	37.9%
	Foreign-born	29.4%	56.0%	76.8%	96.7%	62.1%
Korean	Native and gen 1.5	76.9%	54.0%	28.2%	8.5%	45.1%
	Foreign-born	23.1%	46.0%	71.8%	91.5%	54.9%
Japanese	Native and gen 1.5	66.9%	51.0%	63.8%	73.8%	63.7%
	Foreign-born	33.1%	49.0%	36.2%	26.2%	36.3%
South Asian	Native and gen 1.5	33.9%	16.2%	7.7%	3.7%	18.5%
	Foreign-born	66.1%	83.8%	92.3%	96.3%	81.5%
Southeast Asian–mainland	Native and gen 1.5	72.5%	52.4%	26.6%	6.8%	48.4%
	Foreign-born	27.5%	47.6%	73.4%	93.2%	51.6%
All other Asian	Native and gen 1.5	85.6%	76.4%	64.1%	53.6%	74.8%
	Foreign-born	14.4%	23.6%	35.9%	46.4%	25.2%
Total	Native and gen 1.5	58.1%	41.6%	28.7%	19.7%	40.1%
	Foreign-born	41.9%	58.4%	71.3%	80.3%	59.9%

Source: American Community Survey 2013–17 five-year PUMS.
Note: All Asian Americans ages 25–64 years and employed full-time in the profit and nonprofit sectors.

Table A.4. The Respondents by Graduation Year, Gender, and Asian American Ethnicity

Asian American respondents	1980s college graduates, b. 1958–67	F	M	1990s college graduates, b. 1968–77	F	M	2000s college graduates b. 1978–87	F	M	Total
Chinese American	21	6	15	26	15	11	14	7	7	61
Korean American	8	7	1	8	3	5	12	9	3	28
South Asian American	1	1		2	2		3	2	1	6
Japanese American	4	1	3	1		1	0			5
Vietnamese American	1		1	0			0			1
Filipino American	1		1	0			1	1		2
Total	36	15	21	37	20	17	30	19	11	103

Table A.5. The Types of Colleges Respondents Attended

Asian American workers	Highly selective (Ivy League, Stanford, MIT)	Selective (University of Chicago, NYU, Swarthmore, Haverford, Washington University)	Less selective (SUNY, CUNY, St. John's, Vassar)	Total
Female	26	15	13	54
Male	21	16	12	49
Total	47	31	25	103

Table A.6. Respondents Who Have at Least One Parent with a College Degree

1980s graduates	20
1990s graduates	30
2000s graduates	25

Notes

Introduction

1 Tran, Lee, and Huang 2019; Louie and Wilson-Ahstrom 2018; Gee and Peck 2017; Gee, Peck, and Wong 2015; Chung et al. 2017; Hyun 2005, 2012; Hune 2011; Thatchenkery and Sugiyama 2011; Sy et al. 2010; Kim and Zhao 2014; Lai and Babcock 2013; Chin 2016; Lee and Chin 2015–16.

2 Vault and the Minority Corporate Counsel Association 2018.

3 Gee and Peck 2017.

4 Colby 2017.

5 Green, Holman, and Paskin 2018.

6 Gee and Peck 2018.

7 The lowest annual salary among my interviewees was $95,000.

8 When I say second generation, I also include the 1.5 generation, who entered the United States under the age of thirteen. Moreover, my study primarily focuses on Asian Americans with East Asian heritage. At the time my snowball sample yielded very few South and Southeast Asian Americans.

9 Chua 2011.

10 FindLaw, "Affirmative Action and College Admissions" (2019), https://education.findlaw.com.

11 As a reminder, this was a time for greater diversity on campus, as Yale and Princeton admitted women in 1969. Harvard finally admitted them in 1975. The US Supreme Court heard the *Regents v. Bakke* case in 1978 and ruled that race could be used as a factor but quotas were illegal in admissions. Race as a factor could be used only to support diversity on campus, and the only justification for affirmative action was to enhance the educational benefits of a diverse student body. At the time Justice Harry Blackmun stated, "To ask that this be so is to demand the impossible. In order to get beyond racism, we must first take account of race. There is no other way. And in order to treat some persons equally, we must them differently." Harris (2018).

12 US Census Bureau, Racial Statistics Branch, "Current Population Survey" (2000), www.census.gov; Grieco and Cassidy 2001; National Center for Education Statistics 2017.

13 SEO Scholars, "Program," www.seoscholars.org; Emma Bowen Foundation, http://emmabowenfoundation.com; and POSSE Program, "About Posse," www.possefoundation.org.

Chapter 1. Aspiring Young Asian Americans

1 I alternatively call those children who immigrated before the age of thirteen the 1.5 generation or generation 1.5. Population Reference Bureau, "In the News: Speaking English in the United States" (June 1, 2006), www.prb.org.

2 As mentioned, I used a snowball technique to recruit respondents. My first ring of interviewees was drawn from my college and graduate school alumni networks, and I asked them to introduce me to others who were not part of these networks. During these conversations and preliminary research, three cohorts of second-generation adult Asian Americans emerged, with just seven respondents occupying positions in corner offices. All respondents discussed their families, education, experiences in applying for jobs, networking, moving up career ladders, and occasionally leaving their jobs.

3 See Tables A.1–A.6 in the appendix.

4 The 2018 US Census total population estimate was 327,167,434; the Asian American population estimate was 22,613,335. US Census Bureau, "American FactFinder" (2018), https://factfinder.census.gov.

5 Budiman, Cilluffo, and Ruiz 2019; Lee, Ramakrishnan, and Wong 2018.

6 Budiman, Cilluffo, and Ruiz 2019.

7 Lopez, Ruiz, and Patten 2017.

8 Many Asian American immigrants both past and present are working class and do not have a college degree. For example, see the studies by Erika Lee 2015, Pawan Dhingra 2012, Chin 2005a, Nazli Kibria 1993, Pyong Gap Min 1996, and many others. Working-class immigrants' children are underrepresented in my sample. I believe that most of the children of the working class are in STEM-type jobs.

9 Batalova and Zong 2016.

10 McCarthy 2017.

11 US Bureau of Labor Statistics 2018; Camille L. Ryan and Kurt Bauman, "Educational Attainment in the United States: 2015" (US Census Bureau, 2016), www.census.gov.

12 Lopez, Ruiz, and Patten 2017.

13 Guo 2016.

14 Harris 2004; Kwong and Miščević 2005; Museus and Kiang 2009; Lai and Babcock 2013; Wu 2013; Lee 2015; Zainiddinov 2016.

15 Tran et al. 2018.

16 Kibria 1993; Min 1996; Louie 2004a, 2004b; Chin 2005a, 2005b; Dhingra 2012; Lee 2015.

17 Kochhar and Cilluffo 2018.

18 The respondents are mostly children of college-educated parents.

19 Kwong and Miščević 2005; Lee and Zhou 2015.

20 Tran, Lee, and Huang 2019; Lee and Zhou 2015; Jiménez and Horowitz 2013; Louie 2004a, 2012; Kasinitz et al. 2008; Kibria 2002; Portes and Rumbaut 2001; Gans 1992.

21 Presentation by Jennifer Lee at CUNY Graduate Center 2017.

22 Kasinitz et al. 2005; Rumbaut 2012.

23 To be technically correct, the US-born or native-born category in the census and the American Community Survey includes more than the native-born second generation with immigrant parents, even though many sociologists use this as a proxy for the second generation. Our recent census does not distinguish where the parents of the native born are from. So some of the native-born category include those who are third, fourth, or fifth generation, where their grandparents, great-grandparents, or great-great-grandparents were the first to arrive in the United States. For Asian Americans the third, fourth, and fifth generation numbers are small and thus in my study are included in the second generation definition/calculation.

24 See also Ellen Berrey's 2015 book *The Enigma of Diversity: The Language of Race and the Limits of Racial Justice* for another discussion on affirmative action in higher education. In addition, I write about the importance of affirmative action for Asian Americans in Chin (2019).

25 Green, Holman, and Paskin 2018.

26 Zweigenhaft and Domhoff 2018.

27 Wilson 2018a.

28 Wilson 2018b.

29 See Tran et al. 2018 on hyperselectivity.

30 Kasinitz et al. 2007; Louie 2012; Lee and Zhou 2015; see Crul et al. 2017 on the multiplier effect.

31 Louie 2004a, 2004b.

32 Syed Ali and I are working on a new book, called *The Peer Effect*, on this very topic.

33 Louie 2004b.

34 Louie 2004a, 2012.

35 Kwong and Miščević 2005.

36 Chung 2016.

37 Zhou 1992; Suárez-Orozco, Suárez-Orozco, and Todorova 2008; Louie 2011, 2012.

38 Louie 2011.

39 Lee and Zhou 2015.

40 Louie 2004a.

41 Ayres 1996.

42 De Witt 1990.

43 Kim 2012.

44 Chung 2000.

45 Jessica S. Barnes and Claudette E. Bennett, "The Asian Population: 2000" (US Census Bureau, February 2002), www.census.gov.

46 Borgna Brunner and Beth Rowen, "Timeline of Affirmative Action Milestones" (Infoplease, n.d.), www.infoplease.com.

Chapter 2. The Playbook for Success

1 The Immigration and Nationality Act (Hart-Celler Act) of 1965 changed the racial contours of the American population. Even the term "model minority," coined by William Pettersen, a sociologist at the University of California, Berkeley, in an article in *New York Times Magazine* titled "Success Story, Japanese-American Style," appeared more than fifty years ago, on January 9, 1966. Today the model minority myth is an ubiquitous stereotype: that Asian Americans have collectively achieved occupational success and are not disadvantaged minorities (Harris 2004; Lai and Babcock 2013; Museus and Kiang 2009; Zainiddinov 2016).

2 See Jerry Kang and Kristin Lane's discussion on implicit bias and colorblindness (2010).

3 To many, this is the pervasive model minority myth—see note 1 of this chapter.

4 Gibson 1988; Gans 1992; Kao and Tienda 1995; Waters 1999; Portes and Rumbaut 2001; Suárez-Orozco and Suárez-Orozco 2001.

5 The playbook even reminds immigrant parents that they can persuade their offspring to follow certain plans because of the implicit "immigrant bargain," along with a combination of shaming their children and having bragging rights to their Asian American relatives and friends (Louie 2012). The adult offspring of immigrant parents also feel a commitment to their parents. Regardless of whether their parents are working class or millionaires, the immigrant story is that their parents gave up a great deal to provide a better life for their offspring in the United States. This sentiment is so firmly woven into the playbook that nearly everyone feels the weight of obligation, if not from their own parents, then from their peers. Members of their parents' networks compete ferociously when it comes to bragging about their offspring's success. And if the offspring are lacking in any way, there is no hesitation about shaming the children to bring them into line (Lee and Zhou 2015).

6 Chung 2016; Chen 2019.

7 Zhou 2009.

8 Sue and Sue 1973; Suzuki 1989; Hsia 1988; Hurh and Kim 1989; Hsia and Hirano-Nakanishi 1989; Barringer, Takeuchi, and Xenos 1990; Schneider and Lee 1990; Kim and Chun 1994; Hune and Chan 1997; Bankston and Zhou 2002; Zhou and Xiong 2005; Sakamoto, Goyette, and Kim 2009; Sy et al. 2010; Thatchenkery and Sugiyama 2011; Akutagawa 2013; Zhou, Chin, and Kim 2013; Kiang, Tseng, and Yip 2016; Lopez, Ruiz, and Patten 2017; Lee, Ramakrishnan, and Wong 2018.

9 Kasinitz et al. 2008; Lee and Zhou 2015; Oh 2016.

10 Misra 2014.

11 US Commission on Civil Rights 1992; Tang 1993; Woo 1994, 2000; Gee and Peck 2018; Green, Holman, and Paskin 2018; McGirt 2018.

12 Working hard refers to the belief of many Asian Americans in a growth mind-set, that one can always get better and learn new skills. For example, there is no innate lack of ability that prevents one from working hard and improving, as described Amy Hsin and Yu Xie's 2014 article, "Explaining Asian Americans' Academic Advantage over Whites."

13 Note the debates on quotas and discrimination against Asian American students getting into Ivy League colleges. Many believe that Asian Americans are qualified based largely on their high test scores and grades, but elite colleges and top executive positions have additional criteria. See Gersen 2017.

14 These ideas are usually taught in school (Hsin and Xie 2014).

15 The respondents' parents, who were voluntary immigrants, believed that discrimination against Asian Americans would be temporary and would primarily affect their own generation because they were foreign-born, non–English speakers possessing foreign college degrees or credentials. They believed that discrimination against their children, who were true Americans, having been born and raised in the United States, would be nonexistent or at worst minimal. The interviewees' parents perceived that an education, especially at a prestigious college, along with a concentration in STEM fields, was a safeguard and would eventually lead their children into jobs that would shield them from discrimination. Moreover, since many parents also had degrees in these areas, they were able to actually help their children. This is similar to Pawan Dhingra's work on spelling bees (2018).

16 National Asian American Survey 2017.

17 Some interviewees mentioned that women were also advised to do as instructed.

18 Asian American whiz kids were on the cover of the August 31, 1987, edition of *Time*.

19 Dugger 1992.

20 Alexis Anderson, "Asian American Students Still Struggling with Burden of Expectations," NPR, October 26, 2017, http://diverseeducation.com; Seal 2010; theAsianparent 2017; "When Strict Parenting Becomes an Educational Hindrance" 2011.

21 Chin 2016.

22 The Intel Science Talent Search was formerly known as the Westinghouse Science Talent Search and is currently called the Regeneron Science Talent Search.

23 The playbook includes names of the Ivy League colleges, which, according to the respondents, are some of the only colleges their parents seem to know. The respondents said that having the playbook lulled parents into thinking that it was a simple formula to get into an Ivy League college.

24 Zweigenhaft and Domhoff 1999, 2006, 2011, 2018.

25 Green, Holman, and Paskin 2018.

26 Fiske 2011.

27 Fiske and Dupree 2014; Williams and Dempsey 2014.

Chapter 3. Landing a Job

1 See chapter 1 for information on the American Community Survey 2013–2017 data I used.

2 The Ivy League is an athletic conference comprising eight colleges, but the name also stands for a group of elite colleges from the Northeast and Mid-Atlantic: Dartmouth, Cornell, Harvard, Brown, Yale, Princeton, Columbia, University of

Pennsylvania. These schools remained all male until at least 1969, when Yale and Princeton allowed women on campus. All the rest, except for Columbia, turned coed in the 1970s. Columbia was tightly associated with Barnard, a women's college, and did not turn coed until 1981.

3 I categorized the schools that my respondents attended as Ivy League plus (Ivy League schools, Stanford, MIT), selective (University of Chicago, NYU, University of California system, Swarthmore, Haverford, Washington University, etc.), or less selective (SUNY, St. John's, Vassar, Boston College, CUNY, etc.).

4 Lee and Chin 2015–16.

5 Ho 2009.

6 Dobbin and Kalev 2016, 2017.

Chapter 4. What's in a Promotion?

1 Meyer 2018.

2 Horsager 2012.

3 Chin 2016.

4 Please look at Chimamanda Ngozi Adichie's TED talk on the power of a single story. The "model minority success image" is a single story of Asian Americans that has a life of its own. Asian Americans need to be authentic to counter this—and write their own stories. If we don't someone else will. See Adichie 2009; Sunday Mancini, "3 Lessons from Chimamanda Ngozi Adichie's 'The Danger of a Single Story,'" *Ethos3*, April 11, 2016, www.ethos3.com.

5 Lee 2012.

6 Fiske et al. 2002.

7 I was a witness in the 2018 *SFFA v. Harvard* case, represented by the NAACP Legal Defense Fund supporting Harvard's affirmative action program. The Massachusetts court in October 2019 found that Harvard was not discriminating against Asian American students. The facts show that the number and percentage of Asian Americans admitted have been on an upward trajectory since 1980, so that they represent over 25 percent of the class of 2023. However, the percentage fluctuates up and down every year, which shows a lack of a quota. The personal rating difference is only .05 points. The facts reveal no discrimination in the Harvard admissions office, but as the court ruled, they could do better by implementing bias training. However, as this book reveals, there is discrimination in the work world, maybe among guidance couselors and more. The only way to fix racial discrimination is by addressing race in the admissions policy.

8 Chin et al. 2019; Chin 2019.

9 "Asian American Organizations You Need to Know" 2019.

10 Chin 2016.

Chapter 5. Moving Up to the Corner Office or Close to It

1 Colby 2017.
2 Green, Holman, and Paskin 2018.
3 Caldera 2019.
4 This also raises the question of what professions the first-generation college students have. I suspect that if they are following the playbook, many of them are in STEM-related fields including computer science.
5 Khan 2011; Rivera 2015.
6 Fiske, Cuddy, and Glick 2007.
7 Galinsky et al. 2015.
8 Liu 2016.
9 Zia and Lee 2002.
10 "Japan Buys the Center of New York" 1989; Frail 2017; Stack 2018; Rothman 2017; Perlez 2019.
11 Anderson 2019; Watanabe 2019.

Chapter 6. The Double Bind for Asian American Women

1 US Department of Labor, "Asian American & Pacific Islander Women in the Labor Force," www.dol.gov; Payscale, "The State of the Gender Pay Gap 2019," www.payscale.com.
2 "Asian Women and Men Earned More" 2018.
3 Harwood 2019.
4 Kim and Zhao 2014.
5 Read the writings of Kimberlé Crenshaw (1989), who coined the term "intersectionality."
6 See Yen Le Espiritu's book *Asian American Women and Men: Labor, Laws, and Love* (2007) for how these images are created externally—and thus are not innate to Asian American women—and have persisted over time and morphed.
7 Espiritu explores many of these stereotypes and causes of the images of women (2007).
8 Streitfeld 2015.
9 Guynn 2017; Guynn and Swartz 2017.
10 Gee and Peck 2017.
11 Chung et al. 2017.
12 See examples in Lee and Zhou 2015, 85–88.
13 See more examples in Louie 2004b and Espiritu 2009.
14 Just because the majority of the respondents are not from working-class backgrounds doesn't mean there are not working-class families. There were few who qualified to be in this study. For studies of working-class Asian Americans, see my work on garment workers (Chin 2005), Kwong on Chinatown laborers (2001), and Zhou on Chinatown (2009).
15 Goldman Sachs 2019.

16 Leah 2017; Mac and Alba 2019.

17 Ohlheiser 2017.

18 Guynn and Swartz 2017.

19 Alba 2015.

20 Pao 2017, 87.

21 Among the technology companies in Silicon Valley, Asian Americans represent 47 percent of the workforce yet only 25 percent of all executives (Gee and Peck 2017).

22 There is little research in this area (Buchanan et al. 2018).

23 Cohan 2018; Roscigno 2019.

24 Goldman Sachs 2019.

25 Coaston 2019.

Conclusion

1 Adam Serwer, "What Americans Do Now Will Define Us Forever," *Atlantic*, July 18, 2019, www.theatlantic.com.

2 Michael Luo, "Trump's Racist Tweets, and the Question of Who Belongs in America," *New Yorker*, July 15, 2019, www.newyorker.com.

3 Vivian Louie also discusses this paradox in her books *Compelled to Excel* (2004b) and *Keeping the Immigrant Bargain* (2012). Across the three different immigrant groups (Chinese, Dominicans, and Columbians) there is a seeming paradox. They see the significance of race and experience its ill effects. But they remain remarkably optimistic about their own capabilities to combat racism without institutional support.

4 See Chou and Feagin 2008, 99.

5 Melaku 2019; Pan 2017.

6 Watanabe 2019.

7 Zia and Lee 2002.

8 Although we know that test scores and certain kinds of performance reviews can be racially biased too.

9 DiAngelo 2018.

10 This is the latent discussion in the *SFFA v. Harvard* case that was heard in October 2018; however, based on the data presented, Harvard hasn't discriminated against Asian American students, but there are many other places, including workplaces, that are discriminating against Asian Americans. But in this case Harvard and affirmative action are the targets (Chin et al. 2019).

11 The Coalition for a Diverse Harvard (of which I am a founding board member; see http://diverseharvard.org) along with over twenty other Harvard alumni and student organizations filed an amicus brief with the NAACP Legal Defense Fund to support race-conscious admissions.

12 Chin 2019; Chin et al. 2019; Chin and Ali 2018.

13 Studies by Harvard economics professor Raj Chetty and his team show how important race is to the life trajectories of whites and blacks in our country (Cook 2019). See Opportunity Insights, "Raj Chetty" (2019), https://opportunityinsights.org.

14 Ali and Chin 2018.

15 Eliza Shapiro, "Only 7 Black Students Got into Stuyvesant, N.Y.'s Most Selective High School, Out of 895 Spots," *New York Times*, March 18, 2019, www.nytimes.com.

Bibliography

Adichie, Chimamanda Ngozi. "The Danger of a Single Story." TED, 2009. www.ted.com.

Akutagawa, Linda. "Breaking Stereotypes: An Asian American's View of Leadership Development." *Asian American Journal of Psychology* 4, no. 4 (2013): 277–84.

Alba, Davey. "Ellen Pao Steps Down as CEO after Reddit Revolt." *Wired*, July 10, 2015. www.wired.com.

Alba, Richard, and Guillermo Yrizar Barbosa. "Room at the Top? Minority, Mobility, and the Transition to Democratic Diversity in the USA." *Ethnic and Racial Studies* 39, no. 6 (2015): 917–38.

Ali, Syed, and Margaret M. Chin. "What's Going on with New York's Elite Public High Schools? A Fight over Admissions Is Making All Too Clear the Value of Securing a Seat at One of the City's Finest Schools." *Atlantic*, June 14, 2018.

Anderson, Nick. "Scrutiny of Chinese American Scientists Raises Fears of Ethnic Profiling." *Washington Post*, July 19, 2019. www.washingtonpost.com.

"Asian American Organizations You Need to Know." Diversity Best Practices, April 2019. www.diversitybestpractices.com.

"Asian Women and Men Earned More Than Their White, Black, and Hispanic Counterparts in 2017." *Economics Daily*, 2018. www.bls.gov.

Ayres, B. Drummond. "Affirmative Action Measure Nears a High-Profile Finish." *New York Times*, November 4, 1996. www.nytimes.com.

Bankston, Carl, and Min Zhou. "Being Well vs. Doing Well: Self-Esteem and School Performance among Immigrant and Nonimmigrant Racial and Ethnic Groups." *International Migration Review* 36 (2002): 389–415.

Barringer, Herbert R., David T. Takeuchi, and Peter Xenos. "Education, Occupational Prestige, and Income of Asian Americans." *Sociology of Education* 63, no. 1 (1990): 27–43.

Batalova, Jeanne, and Jie Zong. "Asian Immigrants in the United States." Migration Policy Institute, January 6, 2016. www.migrationpolicy.org.

Bergsieker, Hilary B., Lisa M. Leslie, Vanessa S. Constantine, and Susan T. Fiske. "Stereotyping by Omission: Eliminate the Negative, Accentuate the Positive." *Journal of Personality and Social Psychology* 102, no. 6 (June 2012): 1214–38.

Berrey, Ellen. *The Enigma of Diversity: The Language of Race and the Limits of Racial Justice*. Chicago. University of Chicago Press, 2015.

Buchanan, NiCole T., Settle Isis H., Ivan H. C. Wu, and Diane S. Hayashino. "Sexual Harassment, Racial Harassment, and Well-Being among Asian American Women: An Intersectional Approach." *Women & Therapy* 41, nos. 3–4 (2018): 261–80.

Budiman, Abby, Anthony Cilluffo, and Neil G. Ruiz. "Key Facts about Asian Origin Groups in the U.S." Pew Research Center, May 22, 2019. www.pewresearch.org.

Butler, John K., Jr. "Toward Understanding and Measuring Conditions of Trust: Evolution of a Conditions of Trust Inventory." *Journal of Management* 17, no. 3 (September 1991): 643–63.

Caldera, Camille G. "Asian American, International Admits Accepted Harvard Admissions Offers at Highest Rates." *Harvard Crimson*, May 2019. www.thecrimson.com.

Chang, Sharon. "Searching for Women of Color." *Racism Review*, March 27, 2015. www.racismreview.com.

Chen, Brian. "The Cultural Truth at the Heart of the Lies in 'The Farewell.'" *New York Times*, July 25, 2019.

Chin, Jean Lau, Debra M. Kawahara, and Monica S. Pal. "The Leadership Experiences of Asian Americans." *Asian American Journal of Psychology* 4, no. 4 (2013): 240–48.

Chin, Margaret M. "Asian Americans, Bamboo Ceilings, and Affirmative Action." *Contexts* 15, no. 1 (February 1, 2016): 70–73.

———. "Higher Education Needs More Affirmative Action, Not Less." *Inside Higher Ed*, November 12, 2019. www.insidehighered.com.

———. "Moving On: Chinese Garment Workers after 9/11." In *Wounded City*, edited by Nancy Foner, 184–207. New York: Russell Sage Foundation, 2005b.

———. *Sewing Women: Immigrants and the New York City Garment Industry*. New York: Columbia University Press, 2005a.

Chin, Margaret M., and Syed Ali. "Merit and the Admissions Debates at Harvard University and Stuyvesant High School." *Society Pages*, June 27, 2018. https://thesocietypages.org.

Chin, Margaret M., OiYan Poon, Janelle Wong, and Jerry Park. "Here Are Ten Reasons Not to Fall for the 'Asian American Penalty' Trap in Admissions!" *Medium*, February 2019. https://medium.com.

Chou, Rosalind S., and Joe R. Feagin. *The Myth of the Model Minority: Asian Americans Facing Racism*. Boulder, CO: Paradigm, 2008.

Chua, Amy. *Battle Hymn of the Tiger Mother*. New York: Penguin, 2011.

Chung, Angie Y. *Saving Face: The Emotional Costs of the Asian Immigrant Family Myth*. New Brunswick, NJ: Rutgers University Press, 2016.

Chung, Eric, Samuel Dong, Xiaonan April Hu, Christine Kwon, and Goodwin Liu. "A Portrait of Asian Americans in the Law." SSRN, October 5, 2017. https://papers.ssrn.com.

Chung, Juliet J. "Wen Ho Lee's Daughter Speaks at Forum." *Harvard Crimson*, December 5, 2000. www.thecrimson.com.

Coaston, Jane. "The Intersectionality Wars." *Vox*, 2019. www.vox.com.

Cohan, William D. "Women Say a Rigged System Allows Wall Street to Hide Its Sexual-Harassment Problem." *New Yorker*, January 7, 2018. www.newyorker.com.

Colby, Laura. "Asian Americans Climb the Corporate Ladder, But Only So High." *Bloomberg*, November 21, 2017. www.bloomberg.com.

Cook, Gareth. "The Economist Who Would Fix the American Dream." *Atlantic*, August 2019.

Correll, Shelley, Stephen Benard, and In Paik. "Getting a Job: Is There a Motherhood Penalty?" *American Journal of Sociology* 112, no. 5 (March 2007): 1297–1338.

Crenshaw, Kimberlé. "Demarginalizing the Intersection of Race and Sex: A Black Feminist Critique of Antidiscrimination Doctrine, Feminist Theory and Antiracist Politics." *University of Chicago Legal Forum* 1989, no. 1 (1989): 139–67.

———. *On Intersectionality: Essential Writings*. New York: New Press, 2020.

Crul, Maurice, Jens Schneider, Elif Keskiner, and Frans Lelie. "The Multiplier Effect: How the Accumulation of Cultural and Social Capital Explains Steep Upward Mobility of Children of Low-Educated Immigrants." *Ethnic and Racial Studies* 40 (2017): 321–38.

Cuddy, Amy J. C. *Presence: Bringing Your Boldest Self to Your Biggest Challenges*. New York: Little, Brown, 2015.

Cuddy, Amy J. C., Matthew Kohut, and John Neffinger. "Connect, Then Lead." *Harvard Business Review* 91 (July–August 2013): 54–61.

de Witt, Karen. "Harvard Cleared in Inquiry on Bias." *New York Times*, October 7, 1990. www.nytimes.com.

Dhingra, Pawan. *Life Behind the Lobby: Indian American Motel Owners*. Palo Alto, CA: Stanford University Press, 2012.

———. "What Asian Americans Really Care about When They Care about Education." *Sociological Quarterly* 59, no. 2 (2018): 301–19.

DiAngelo, Robin. *White Fragility: Why It's So Hard for White People to Talk about Racism*. Boston: Beacon, 2018.

Dobbin, Frank, and Alexandra Kalev. "Are Diversity Programs Merely Ceremonial?" In *The Sage Handbook of Organizational Institutionalism*, edited by Royston Greenwood, Christine Oliver, Thomas B. Lawrence, and Renate E. Meyer, 808–28. Thousand Oaks, CA: Sage, 2017.

———. "Why Diversity Programs Fail." *Harvard Business Review*, July–August 2016.

Dugger, Celia W. "U.S. Study Says Asian-Americans Face Widespread Discrimination." *New York Times*, February 29, 1992. www.nytimes.com.

Espiritu, Yen Le. *Asian American Women and Men: Labor, Laws, and Love*. 2nd ed. Lanham, MD: Rowman & Littlefield, 2007.

———. "Emotions, Sex, and Money: The Lives of Filipino Children of Immigrants." In *Across Generations: Immigrant Families in America*, edited by Nancy Foner, 47–71. New York: New York University Press, 2009.

Feliciano, Cynthia, and Yader R. Lanuza. "An Immigrant Paradox? Contextual Attainment and Intergenerational Educational Mobility." *American Sociological Review* 82, no. 1 (2017): 211–41.

Fiske, Susan T. *Envy Up, Scorn Down*. New York: Russell Sage Foundation, 2011. www.russellsage.org.

———. "Managing Ambivalent Prejudices: Smart-but-Cold and Warm-but-Dumb Stereotypes." *Annals of the American Academy of Political and Social Science* 639, no. 1 (2012): 33–48.

———. "Stereotype Content: Warmth and Competence Endure." *Current Directions in Psychological Science* 27, no. 2 (2018): 67–73.

Fiske, Susan T., Amy J. C. Cuddy, and Peter Glick. "Universal Dimensions of Social Cognition: Warmth and Competence." *Trends in Cognitive Sciences* 11, no. 2 (2007): 77–83.

Fiske, Susan T., Amy J. C. Cuddy, Peter Glick, and Jun Xu. "A Model of (Often Mixed) Stereotype Content: Competence and Warmth Respectively Follow from Perceived Status and Competition." *Journal of Personality and Social Psychology* 82, no. 6 (June 2002): 878–902.

Fiske, Susan T., and Cydney Dupree. "Gaining Trust as Well as Respect in Communicating to Motivated Audiences about Science Topics." *Proceedings of the National Academy of Sciences* 111, suppl. 4 (2014): 13593–97.

Frail, T. A. "The Injustice of Japanese-American Internment Camps Resonates Strongly to This Day." *Smithsonian*, January 2017. www.smithsonianmag.com.

Friedman, Sam, and Daniel Laurison. *The Class Ceiling: Why It Pays to Be Privileged.* Bristol: Policy Press, 2019.

Galinsky, Adam D., Andrew R. Todd, Astrid C. Homan, Katherine W. Phillips, Evan P. Apfelbaum, Stacey J. Sasaki, Jennifer Richeson, Jennifer Olayon, and William Maddux. "Maximizing the Gains and Minimizing the Pains of Diversity: A Policy Perspective." *Perspectives on Psychological Science* 10 (2015): 742–48.

Gans, Herbert J. "Second-Generation Decline: Scenarios for the Economic and Ethnic Futures of the Post-1965 American Immigrants." *Ethnic and Racial Studies* 15, no. 2 (April 1, 1992): 173–92.

Gee, Buck, and Denise Peck. "Asian Americans Are the Least Likely Group in the U.S. to Be Promoted to Management." *Harvard Business Review*, May 31, 2018. https://hbr.org.

———. "The Illusion of Asian Success: Scant Progress for Minorities in Cracking the Glass Ceiling From 2007–2015." Ascend Foundation, 2017.

Gee, Buck, Denise Peck, and Janet Wong. "Hidden in Plain Sight: Asian American Leaders in Silicon Valley." Ascend Foundation, May 2015.

Gersen, Jeannie Suk. "The Uncomfortable Truth about Affirmative Action and Asian-Americans." *New Yorker*, August 2017. www.newyorker.com.

Gibson, Margaret A. *Accommodation without Assimilation.* Ithaca, NY: Cornell University Press. 1988.

Goldman Sachs. "Goldman Sachs | Professionals." 2019. www.goldmansachs.com.

Green, Jeff, Jordyn Holman, and Janet Paskin. "America's C-suites Keep Getting Whiter (and More Male Too)." *Bloomberg Businessweek*, September 21, 2018. www.bloomberg.com.

Greenman, Emily, and Yu Xie. "Double Jeopardy? The Interaction of Gender and Race on Earnings in the United States." *Social Forces* 86, no. 3 (March 2008): 1217–44.

Grieco, Elizabeth M., and Rachel C. Cassidy. "Overview of Race and Hispanic Origin: Census 2000 Brief." US Census Bureau, 2001. www.census.gov.

Guo, Jeff. "The Asian American 'Advantage' That Is Actually an Illusion." *Washington Post*, December 29, 2016. www.washingtonpost.com.

Guynn, Jessica. "It's Called the 'Pao Effect'—Asian Women in Tech Are Fighting Deep-Rooted Discrimination." *USA Today*, September 19, 2017. www.usatoday.com.

Guynn, Jessica, and Jon Swartz. "Sexual Harassment Scandal Shakes Insular, Influential Venture Capital World." *USA Today*, June 29, 2017. www.usatoday.com.

Harris, Adam. "The Supreme Court Justice Who Forever Changed Affirmative Action." *Atlantic*, October 13, 2018.

Harris, Michelle. "Racial and Ethnic Diversity in Perceptions of Discrimination." *Sociological Imagination* 40, no. 2 (2004): 65–89.

Harvard University. "Harvard Admissions Lawsuit." 2019. https://admissionscase.harvard.edu.

Harwood, Morgan. "Equal Pay for Asian American and Pacific Islander Women." National Women's Law Center, March 2019. https://nwlc-ciw49tixgw5lbab.stackpathdns.com.

Ho, Karen Zouwen. *Liquidated: An Ethnography of Wall Street*. Durham, NC: Duke University Press, 2009.

Horsager, David. "You Can't Be a Great Leader without Trust—Here's How You Build It." *Forbes Leadership Forum*, October 24, 2012. www.forbes.com.

Hsia, Jayjia. *Asian Americans in Higher Education and at Work*. Hillsdale, NJ: Lawrence Erlbaum, 1988.

Hsia, Jayjia, and Marsha Hirano-Nakanishi. "The Demographics of Diversity: Asian Americans and Higher Education." *Change* 21, no. 6 (1989): 20–27.

Hsin, Amy, and Yu Xie. "Explaining Asian Americans' Academic Advantage over Whites." *PNAS* 111, no. 23 (2014): 8416–21.

Hune, Shirley. "Asian American Woman Faculty and the Contested Space of the Classroom: Navigating Student Resistance and (Re)claiming Authority and Their Rightful Place." In *Women of Color in Higher Education: Turbulent Past, Promising Future*, edited by Gaëtane Jean-Marie and Brenda Lloyd-Jones, 307–35. Bingley: Emerald, 2011.

Hune, Shirley, and Kenyon S. Chan. "Special Focus: Asian Pacific American Demographic and Educational Trends." In *Fifteenth Annual Status Report on Minorities in Higher Education, 1996–1997*, edited by Deborah J. Carter and Reginald Wilson, 1–63. Washington, DC: American Council on Education, 1997.

Hurh, Won Moo, and Kwang Chung Kim. "The 'Success' Image of Asian Americans: Its Validity, and Its Practical and Theoretical Implications." *Ethnic & Racial Studies* 12, no. 4 (October 1989): 512–38.

Hyun, Jane. *Breaking the Bamboo Ceiling: Career Strategies for Asians*. New York: Harper Business, 2005.

———. "Leadership Principles for Capitalizing on Culturally Diverse Teams: The Bamboo Ceiling Revisited." *Leader to Leader* 2012, no. 64 (2012): 14–19.

"Japan Buys the Center of New York." *New York Times*, November 3, 1989. www.nytimes.com.

Jiménez, Tomás R., and Adam L. Horowitz. "When White Is Just Alright: How Immigrants Redefine Achievement and Reconfigure the Ethnoracial Hierarchy." *American Sociological Review* 78, no. 5 (October 1, 2013): 849–71.

Judd, Charles Mosley, Laurie James-Hawkins, Vincent Yzerbyt, and Yoshihisa Kashima. "Fundamental Dimensions of Social Judgment: Understanding the Relations between Judgments of Competence and Warmth." *Journal of Personality and Social Psychology* 89, no. 6 (2005): 899–913.

Kang, Jerry, and Kristin Lane. "Seeing through Colorblindness: Implicit Bias and the Law." *UCLA Law Review* 58, no. 465 (2010).

Kang, Miliann. *The Managed Hand: Race, Gender, and the Body in Beauty Service Work*. Berkeley: University of California Press. 2010.

Kao, Grace, and Marta Tienda. "Optimism and Achievement: The Educational Performance of Immigrant Youth." *Social Science Quarterly* 76, no. 1 (1995): 1–19.

Kasinitz, Philip, John H. Mollenkopf, Mary C. Waters, and Jennifer Holdaway. *Inheriting the City: The Children of Immigrants Come of Age*. New York: Russell Sage Foundation, 2008.

Kent, Mary, and Robert Lalasz. "In the News: Speaking English in the United States." Population Reference Bureau, June 1, 2006. www.prb.org.

Khan, Shamus Rahman. *Privilege: The Making of an Adolescent Elite at St. Paul's School*. Princeton, NJ: Princeton University Press, 2011.

Kiang, Lisa, Vivian Tseng, and Tiffany Yip. "Placing Asian American Child Development within Historical Context." *Child Development* 87, no. 4 (2016): 995–1013.

Kibria, Nazli. *Becoming Asian American: Second Generation Chinese and Korean American Identities*. Baltimore: Johns Hopkins University Press, 2002.

———. *Family Tightrope: The Changing Lives of Vietnamese Americans*. Princeton, NJ: Princeton University Press, 1993.

Kim, ChangHwan, and Yang Zhao. "Are Asian American Women Advantaged? Labor Market Performance of College Educated Female Workers." *Social Forces* 93, no. 2 (2014): 623–52.

Kim, Marlene. "Unfairly Disadvantaged? Asian Americans and Unemployment during and after the Great Recession (2007–10)." Economic Policy Institute, April 5, 2012. www.epi.org.

Kim, Uichol, and Maria B. J. Chun. "Educational 'Success' of Asian Americans: An Indigenous Perspective." *Journal of Applied Developmental Psychology* 15, no. 3 (1994): 329–39.

Kochhar, Rakesh, and Anthony Cilluffo. "Income Inequality in the U.S. Is Rising Most Rapidly among Asians." Pew Research Center, July 12, 2018. www.pewsocialtrends.org.

Kwong, Peter. *Chinatown, New York: Labor and Politics, 1930–1950*. Rev. ed. New York: New Press, 2001.

Kwong, Peter, and Dušanka Dušana Miščević. *Chinese America: The Untold Story of America's Oldest New Community*. New York: New Press, 2005.

Lai, Lei, and Linda C. Babcock. "Asian Americans and Workplace Discrimination: The Interplay between Sex of Evaluators and the Perception of Social Skills." *Journal of Organizational Behavior* 34, no. 3 (2013): 310–26.

Leah, Rachel. "Hollywood's Brightest Join the 10-Year-Old #MeToo Movement, but Will That Change Anything?" *Salon*, October 17, 2017.

Lee, Erika. *The Making of Asian America: A History*. New York: Simon & Schuster, 2015.

Lee, Hyein, and Margaret M. Chin. "Navigating the Road to Work: Second-Generation Asian American Finance Workers." *Asian American Policy Review* 26 (2015–16): 20–29.

Lee, Jennifer. "Stereotype Promise." *RSF Blog*, 2012. www.russellsage.org.

Lee, Jennifer, Karthick Ramakrishnan, and Janelle Wong. "Accurately Counting Asian Americans Is a Civil Rights Issue." *Annals of the American Academy of Political and Social Science* 677, no. 1 (May 1, 2018): 191–202.

Lee, Jennifer, and Min Zhou. *The Asian American Achievement Paradox*. New York: Russell Sage, 2015.

Liu, Lowen. "Just the Wrong Amount of American." *Slate*, September 2016. https://slate.com.

Lopez, Gustavo, Neil G. Ruiz, and Eileen Patten. "Key Facts about Asian Americans." Pew Research Center, September 8, 2017. www.pewresearch.org.

Louie, Vivian. "'Being Practical' or 'Doing What I Want': The Role of Parents in the Academic Choices of Chinese Americans." In *Becoming New Yorkers: Ethnographies of the New Second Generation*, edited by Philip Kasinitz, John H. Mollenkopf, and Mary C. Waters, 79–110. New York: Russell Sage Foundation, 2004a.

———. *Compelled to Excel: Immigration, Education, and Opportunity among Chinese Americans*. Stanford, CA: Stanford University Press, 2004b.

———. "Complicating the Story of Immigrant Integration." In *Writing Immigration: Scholars and Journalists in Dialogue*, edited by Marcelo Suarez-Orozco, Vivian Louie, and Roberto Suro, 219–35. Berkeley: University of California Press, 2011.

———. *Keeping the Immigrant Bargain: The Costs and Rewards of Success in America*. New York: Russell Sage Foundation, 2012.

Louie, Vivian, and Alicia Wilson-Ahstrom. "Moving It Forward: The Power of Mentoring, and How Universities Can Confront Institutional Barriers Facing Junior Researchers of Color." William T. Grant Foundation, September 2018. https://eric.ed.gov.

Mac, Ryan, and Davey Alba. "These Tech Execs Faced #MeToo Allegations. They All Have New Jobs." *BuzzFeed News*, April 16, 2019. www.buzzfeednews.com.

McCarthy, Niall. "India and China Accounted for 82% of U.S. H-1B Visas in 2016." *Forbes*, April 19, 2017. www.forbes.com.

McGirt, Ellen. "Race Ahead, the Asian Glass Ceiling." *Fortune*, June 4, 2018. https://fortune.com.

Melaku, Tsedale M. *You Don't Look Like a Lawyer: Black Women and Systemic Gendered Racism*. New York: Rowman & Littlefield, 2019.

Meyer, Eileen Hoenigman. "Sponsors vs. Mentors: What's the Difference & Why It Matters." *Glassdoor Blog*, January 31, 2018. www.glassdoor.com.

Min, Pyong Gap. *Caught in the Middle: Korean Communities in New York and Los Angeles*. Berkeley: University of California Press, 1996.

Misra, Tanvi. "Asian-American Leadership Programs Tackle the 'Bamboo Ceiling.'" *Code Switch*, July 7, 2014. www.npr.org.

Museus, Samuel D., and Peter Kiang. "Deconstructing the Model Minority Myth and How It Contributes to the Invisible Minority Reality in Higher Education Research." *New Directions for Institutional Research* 142 (2009): 5–15.

National Asian American Survey. May 16, 2017. http://naasurvey.com.

National Center for Education Statistics. "Digest of Education Statistics. Table 101.20, Estimates of Resident Population, by Race/Ethnicity and Age Group: Selected Years 1980–2017." 2017. www.nces.ed.gov.

Oh, Joong Hwan. *Immigration and Social Capital in the Age of Social Media*. Lanham, MD: Lexington Books, 2016.

Ohlheiser, Abby. "The Woman behind 'Me Too' Knew the Power of the Phrase When She Created It—10 Years Ago." *Washington Post*, October 19, 2017. www.washingtonpost.com.

Pan, Yung-Yi Diana. *Incidental Racialization: Performative Assimilation in Law School*. Philadelphia: Temple University Press, 2017.

Pao, Ellen. *Reset: My Fight for Inclusion and Lasting Change*. New York: Spiegel & Grau, 2017.

Perlez, Jane. "F.B.I. Bars Some China Scholars from Visiting U.S. over Spying Fears." *New York Times*, April 14, 2019. www.nytimes.com.

Pettersen, William. "Success Story, Japanese-American Style." *New York Times Magazine*, January 9, 1966. www.nytimes.com.

Portes, Alejandro, and Ruben G. Rumbaut. *Legacies: The Story of the Immigrant Second Generation*. Berkeley: University of California Press, 2001.

Posse Foundation. "The Posse Foundation: Celebrating 30 Years of Scholar Success." www.possefoundation.org.

Rivera, Lauren A. "Gender and Race Inequality in Management: Critical Issues, New Evidence: Diversity within Reach: Recruitment versus Hiring in Elite Firms." *Annals of the American Academy of Political and Social Science* 639 (2012): 71–258.

———. *Pedigree: How Elite Students Get Elite Jobs*. Princeton, NJ: Princeton University Press, 2015.

Roscigno, Vincent J. "Discrimination, Sexual Harassment, and the Impact of Workplace Power." *Socius: Sociological Research for a Dynamic World* 5 (2019): 1–21.

Roth, Louise Marie. *Selling Women Short: Gender and Money on Wall Street.* Princeton, NJ: Princeton University Press, 2006.

Rothman, Lily. "Vietnam War Enemies Exposed: This Week in History." *Time*, August 21, 2017. https://time.com.

Rousseau, Denise M., Sim B. Sitkin, Ronald S. Burt, and Colin F. Camerer. "Not So Different After All: A Cross-Discipline View of Trust." *Academy of Management Review* 23, no. 3 (June 1998): 393–404.

Rumbaut, R. G. "Generation 1.5: Educational Experiences." 2012. https://escholarship.org.

Sakamoto, Arthur, Kimberly A. Goyette, and Chang Hwan Kim. "Socioeconomic Attainments of Asian Americans." *Annual Review of Sociology* 35 (2009): 255–76.

Schmidt, Eric, Jonathan Rosenberg, and Alan Eagle. *Trillion Dollar Coach: The Leadership Playbook of Silicon Valley's Bill Campbell.* New York: HarperCollins, 2019.

Schneider, Barbara, and Yongsook Lee. "A Model for Academic Success: The School and Home Environment of East Asian Students." *Anthropology & Education Quarterly* 21, no. 4 (1990): 358–77.

Seal, Kathy. "Asian-American Parenting and Academic Success." *Pacific Standard*, December 13, 2010. https://psmag.com.

Smith, Robert C. *Mexican New York: Transnational Lives of New Immigrants.* Berkeley: University of California Press, 2006.

Stack, Liam. "Korean War, a 'Forgotten' Conflict That Shaped the Modern World—The New York Times." *New York Times*, 2018. www.nytimes.com.

Steele, Claude M., and Joshua Aronson. "Stereotype Threat and the Intellectual Test Performance of African Americans." *Journal of Personality and Social Psychology* 69, no. 5 (1995): 797–811.

Streitfeld, David. "Ellen Pao Loses Silicon Valley Bias Case Against Kleiner Perkins." *New York Times*, March 27, 2015. www.nytimes.com.

Suárez-Orozco, Carola. *Children of Immigration.* Cambridge, MA: Harvard University Press, 2001.

Suárez-Orozco, Carola, Marcelo M. Suárez-Orozco, and Irina Todorova. *Learning a New Land: Immigrant Students in American Society.* Cambridge, MA: Belknap, 2008.

Sue, Derald Wing, and David Sue. "Understanding Asian-Americas: The Neglected Minority." *Personnel and Guidance Journal* 51, no. 6 (1973): 386–89.

Suzuki, Bob. "Asian Americans as the 'Model Minority': Outdoing Whites? Or Media Hype?" *Change*, November–December 1989, 13–19.

Sy, Thomas, Lynn Shore, Judy Strauss, Ted Shore, Susanna Tram, Paul Whiteley, and Kristine Ikeda-Muromachi. "Leadership Perceptions as a Function of Race-Occupation Fit: The Case of Asian Americans." *Journal of Applied Psychology* 95, no. 5 (2010): 902–19.

Takei, Isao, Arthur Sakamoto, and Janet Kuo. "Managerial Attainment of College-Educated, Native-Born Asian Americans." *Global Journal of Interdisciplinary Social Sciences* September–October 2014. www.longdom.org.

Tang, Joyce. "The Career Attainment of Caucasian and Asian Engineers." *Sociological Quarterly* 34, no. 3 (1993): 467–96.

Thatchenkery, Tojo, and Keimei Sugiyama. *Making the Invisible Visible: Understanding Leadership Contributions of Asian Minorities in the Workplace*. New York: Palgrave Macmillan, 2011.

theAsianparent. "The Difference between an Asian Parent and a Western One." February 17, 2017. https://sg.theasianparent.com.

Tran, Van C., Jennifer Lee, and Tiffany Huang. "Revisiting the Asian Second-Generation Advantage." *Ethnic and Racial Studies* 42 (2019): 2248–69.

Tran, Van C., Jennifer Lee, Oshin Khachikian, and Jess Lee. "Hyper-selectivity, Racial Mobility, and the Remaking of Race." *RSF: The Russell Sage Foundation Journal of the Social Sciences* 4, no. 5 (2018): 188–209.

Tuan, Mia. *Forever Foreigners or Honorary Whites? The Asian Ethnic Experience Today*. New Brunswick, NJ: Rutgers University Press, 1998.

US Bureau of Labor Statistics. "Labor Force Characteristics by Race and Ethnicity, 2017." BLS Reports, August 2018. www.bls.gov.

US Census Bureau. "American Community Survey Data." 2017. www.census.gov.

US Commission on Civil Rights. "Civil Rights Issues Facing Asian Americans in the 1990s." February 1992. www.ncjrs.gov.

Valian, Virginia. *Why So Slow? The Advancement of Women*. Cambridge, MA: MIT Press, 1999.

Vault and the Minority Corporate Counsel Association. "Vault/MCCA Law Firm Diversity Survey 2018 Report." 2018. www.mcca.com.

Warikoo, Natasha K. *The Diversity Bargain: And Other Dilemmas of Race, Admissions, and Meritocracy at Elite Universities*. Chicago: University of Chicago Press, 2016.

Watanabe, Teresa. "Is This Police Work of Racial Profiling? U.S. Crackdown Puts Chinese Scholars on Edge." *Los Angeles Times*, July 22, 2019.

Waters, Mary. *Black Identities: West Indian Immigrant Dreams and American Realities*. Cambridge, MA: Harvard University Press, 1999.

"When Strict Parenting Becomes an Educational Hindrance." *8Asians*, September 6, 2011. www.8asians.com.

Williams, Joan C., and Rachel Dempsey. *What Works for Women at Work: Four Patterns Working Women Need to Know*. New York: New York University Press, 2014.

Wilson, Valerie. "10 Years after the Start of the Great Recession, Black and Asian Households Have Yet to Recover Lost Income." *Working Economics Blog*, September 12, 2018a. www.epi.org.

———. "Digging into the 2017 ACS: Improved Income Growth for Native Americans, but Lots of Variation in the Pace of Recovery for Different Asian Ethnic Groups." *Working Economics Blog*, September 14, 2018b. www.epi.org.

Woo, Deborah. *Glass Ceilings and Asian Americans: The New Face of Workplace Barriers*. Walnut Creek, CA: AltaMira, 2000.

———. *The Glass Ceiling and Asian Americans*. US Department of Labor, Glass Ceiling Commission, 1994.

Wu, Ellen. *The Color of Success: Asian Americans and the Origins of the Model Minority*. Princeton, NJ: Princeton University Press, 2013.

Zainiddinov, Hakim. "Racial and Ethnic Differences in Perceptions of Discrimination among Muslim Americans." *Ethnic and Racial Studies* 39, no. 15 (2016): 2701–21.

Zhou, Min. *Chinatown: The Socioeconomic Potential of an Urban Enclave*. Philadelphia: Temple University Press, 1992.

———. "How Neighborhoods Matter for Immigrant Children: The Formation of Educational Resources in Chinatown, Koreatown, and Pico Union, Los Angeles." *Journal of Ethnic and Migration Studies* 35, no. 7 (2009): 1153–79.

Zhou, Min, and Carl L. Bankston III. "Family Pressure and the Educational Experience of the Daughters of Vietnamese Refugees." *International Migration* 39, no. 4 (2001): 133–51.

Zhou, Min, and Guoxuan Cai. "Chinese Language Media in the United States: Immigration and Assimilation in American Life." *Qualitative Sociology* 25, no. 3 (2002): 419–41.

Zhou, Min, and Margaret M. Chin, and Rebecca Kim. "The Transformation of Chinese America: New York vs. Los Angeles." In *New York and Los Angeles: The Uncertain Future*, edited by David Halle and Andrew A. Beveridge, 358–84. Oxford: Oxford University Press. 2013.

Zhou, Min, and Yang Sao Xiong. "The Multifaceted American Experiences of the Children of Asian Immigrants: Lessons for Segmented Assimilation." *Ethnic and Racial Studies* 28, no. 6 (November 1, 2005): 1119–52.

Zia, Helen, and Wen Ho Lee. *My Country versus Me: The First Hand Account by the Los Alamos Scientist Who Was Falsely Accused of Being a Spy*. New York: Hachette Books, 2002.

Zweigenhaft, Richard, and G. William Domhoff. *Diversity in the Power Elite: Have Women and Minorities Reached the Top?* New Haven, CT: Yale University Press, 1999.

———. *Diversity in the Power Elite: How It Happened, Why It Matters*. Lanham, MD: Rowman & Littlefield, 2006.

———. *Diversity in the Power Elite: Ironies and Unfulfilled Promises*. 3rd ed. Lanham, MD: Rowman & Littlefield, 2018.

———. *The New CEOs: Women, African American, Latino, and Asian American Leaders of Fortune 500 Companies*. Lanham, MD: Rowman & Littlefield, 2011.

Index

About the Author

MARGARET M. CHIN was born and raised in New York City and is herself a child of Chinese immigrant parents. She's a first-generation college student and an affirmative action recipient. She received her BA from Harvard University and her PhD from Columbia University. She is Professor of Sociology at Hunter College and the Graduate Center, Faculty Associate of the Hunter College Roosevelt House Public Policy Institute, and affiliated with the Hunter College Asian American Studies Program. Her honors include an American Sociological Association's Minority Fellows Award, an NSF Dissertation Grant, a Social Science Research Council Postdoctoral Fellowship in International Migration, and a Woodrow Wilson Foundation Fellowship for junior faculty. She was the Vice President of the Eastern Sociological Society (2015–2016). Her specialties include immigration, family, work, education, Asian Americans, and children of immigrants. She authored *Sewing Women: Immigrants and the New York City Garment Industry*, an illuminating ethnography on the Chinese and Korean garment sectors, which received an Honorable Mention from the Thomas and Znaniecki Annual Book Award for best book on Immigration from the ASA International Migration Section. She's currently working on a manuscript tentatively titled *The Peer Effect: How to Build Better Schools and Improve Our Educational System*. She testified as one of the amici supporting Harvard's race-conscious admissions program. She is on the board of the Tenement Museum and also a founding board member of the Coalition for a Diverse Harvard, a mostly alumni group working for diversity at Harvard.